U.S.-China Security Management

Assessing the Military-to-Military Relationship

KEVIN POLLPETER

Prepared for the United States Air Force

PROJECT AIR FORCE

The research reported here was sponsored by the United States Air Force under Contract F49642-01-C-0003. Further information may be obtained from the Strategic Planning Division, Directorate of Plans, Hq USAF.

Library of Congress Cataloging-in-Publication Data

Pollpeter, Kevin.
   U.S.–China security management : assessing the military-to-military relationship / Kevin Pollpeter.
      p. cm.
   "MG-143."
   Includes bibliographical references.
   ISBN 0-8330-3536-3 (pbk. : alk. paper)
   1. United States—Military relations—China. 2. China—Military relations—United States. I. Title.

UA835.P59 2004
355'.031'09730951—dc22

2004004374

The RAND Corporation is a nonprofit research organization providing objective analysis and effective solutions that address the challenges facing the public and private sectors around the world. RAND's publications do not necessarily reflect the opinions of its research clients and sponsors.

RAND® is a registered trademark.

Published 2004 by the RAND Corporation
1700 Main Street, P.O. Box 2138, Santa Monica, CA 90407-2138
1200 South Hayes Street, Arlington, VA 22202-5050
201 North Craig Street, Suite 202, Pittsburgh, PA 15213-1516
RAND URL: http://www.rand.org/
To order RAND documents or to obtain additional information, contact
Distribution Services: Telephone: (310) 451-7002;
Fax: (310) 451-6915; Email: order@rand.org

Preface

Controversy has surrounded the United States military-to-military relationship with China ever since rapprochement began in 1971. The current debate on Department of Defense activities with the People's Liberation Army (PLA) have focused attention on the value, rationale, and benefits of the relationship. This study documents the history of U.S. security management with China from 1971 to the present and, based on that history, examines the arguments for and against conducting certain types of activities with the PLA. It then recommends a program of suitable military-to-military activities based on prescribed constraints and goals.

The research reported here was sponsored by the Deputy Chief of Staff for Air and Space Operations, U.S. Air Force (AF/XO), and the Commander, Pacific Air Forces (PACAF/CC), and conducted in the Strategy and Doctrine Program of RAND Project AIR FORCE. The report should be of value to the national security community and interested members of the general public, especially those concerned with U.S. relations in the Asia-Pacific region. Comments are welcome and should be sent to the project leader, James Mulvenon, or the RAND Project AIR FORCE acting director of the Strategy and Doctrine Program, Alan Vick:

James C. Mulvenon
1200 South Hayes St.
Arlington, VA 22202
(703) 413-1100 x5225
mulvenon@rand.org

Alan Vick
1200 South Hayes St.
Arlington, VA 22202
(703) 413-1100 x5253
alanv@rand.org

RAND Project Air Force

RAND Project AIR FORCE (PAF), a division of the RAND Corporation, is the U.S. Air Force's federally funded research and development center for studies and analyses. PAF provides the Air Force with independent analyses of policy alternatives affecting the development, employment, combat readiness, and support of current and future aerospace forces. Research is performed in four programs: Aerospace Force Development; Manpower, Personnel, and Training; Resource Management; and Strategy and Doctrine.

Additional information about PAF is available on our web site at http://www.rand.org/paf.

The RAND Corporation Quality Assurance Process

Peer review is an integral part of all RAND research projects. Prior to publication, this document, as with all documents in the RAND monograph series, was subject to a quality assurance process to ensure that the research meets several standards, including the following: The problem is well formulated; the research approach is well designed and well executed; the data and assumptions are sound; the findings are useful and advance knowledge; the implications and recommendations follow logically from the findings and are explained thoroughly; the documentation is accurate, understandable, cogent, and temperate in tone; the research demonstrates understanding of related previous studies; and the research is relevant, objective, independent, and balanced. Peer review is conducted by research professionals who were not members of the project team.

RAND routinely reviews and refines its quality assurance process and also conducts periodic external and internal reviews of the quality of this body of work. For additional details regarding the RAND quality assurance process, visit http://www.rand.org/standards/.

Contents

Tables

Summary

U.S.-China military relations are at an important crossroads. Because of failures in the U.S.-China military relationship and the relationship's perceived lack of ability to produce tangible benefits, many observers have come to doubt its value and even argue that the relationship has harmed U.S. national security. In 2001, the Defense Department began a reassessment of its relations with the People's Liberation Army (PLA) to determine the extent and appropriate nature of these contacts. This reevaluation of the U.S.-China military relationship led to a severe curtailment in military-to-military activities. Since the EP-3 incident in April 2001, all military-to-military activities with the PLA were reviewed on a case-by-case basis pending the completion of a policy review. The few exchanges that do take place are mainly military education exchanges and high-level dialogue. The completion of the policy review and the holding of Defense Consultative Talks in December 2002 have now opened the door for military-to-military contacts to expand.

This report examines the debate surrounding U.S.-China security cooperation and concludes that security cooperation between the United States and China has value. Because of the possibility of armed conflict over Taiwan, the United States needs to maintain a military-to-military relationship with China. The military relationship with the PLA is heavily constrained, however, in the benefits it can provide the U.S. military. Consequently, conducting the type and degree of military-to-military activities with the PLA that have been conducted in the past is not appropriate. This study argues that the

U.S. military-to-military relationship with China should not focus on security cooperation. Instead, it should focus on security management in which dialogue, information gathering, and limited cooperation take place to minimize misperceptions and the chances of conflict.

Different Approaches

A significant hindrance in developing U.S.-China military relations is the fundamentally opposite approach each side uses in pursuing co-operative relationships. The U.S. military prefers a bottom-up approach in which lower-level contacts build trust and identify areas of common interest. Once identified, these areas can be built upon with more in-depth cooperation. The PLA, on the other hand, prefers a top-down approach in which higher-level dialogue is employed to build trust, which is a stepping stone to identify and reach areas of agreement. Without this trust and agreement on strategic issues, the PLA is uncomfortable with further enhancing cooperation.

U.S.-China military relations are also constrained by significant policy differences between China and the United States over core security concerns, such as Taiwan and U.S. activism. The United States remains wary of China's refusal to renounce force to unify with Taiwan. China, for its part, resents the U.S. global force posture, use of force, and continued military assistance to Taiwan, which are seen as efforts to undermine China's sovereignty and security. As a result of these policy differences, each side regards the other side as a potential enemy. Consequently, the PLA has been reluctant to be equally transparent in its relations with the U.S. military, despite agreement on military-to-military activities at the presidential level. (See pages 80–86.)

Four Issues of Contention

The current debate in the United States on U.S.-China military relations has centered around four major issues of contention: the potential risk of U.S.-China military relations to U.S. national security, the potential benefits of the U.S.-China military relationship to the United States, the ability of the United States to influence China, and the relative levels of reciprocity and transparency in the relationship.

Benefits for the PLA?

Whether the PLA has benefited from its relationship with the U.S. military can largely be determined only through inference. Much information about U.S. military strategy and doctrine is available from open sources, including the Internet, making it entirely possible that considerable PLA knowledge of the U.S. military has come from a massive translation effort that has disseminated U.S. writings widely within the organization. It is also possible, however, that questions asked by PLA delegations to their U.S. interlocutors could have provided greater insight or cleared up misperceptions regarding U.S. doctrine. An additional measure of whether the PLA benefits from its interactions with the U.S. military is its own opinion of the value of the relationship. The PLA reportedly values its relationship with the U.S. military because it can draw lessons on how it should conduct reform. Thus, it must be assumed that the PLA has benefited to some extent from its relationship with the U.S. military. (See pages 43–47.)

Benefits to the United States?

In contrast, some observers contend that the U.S. military has not benefited from its relationship with the PLA because of the latter's penchant for secrecy and deception. Again, it is difficult to assess from open sources the benefit of the relationship for the U.S. military. Interlocutors, however, have provided specific examples of instances where information was gathered on the PLA through delegation visits or through the normal function of the attaché office, indicating that the U.S. military has benefited to some extent from its relationship with the PLA. (See page 47.)

Military-to-Military as a Tool of Influence?

A case study examination of the U.S.-China relationship in regard to military-to-military relations, intellectual property rights, and arms control and nonproliferation indicates that the United States has limited influence over China. Influence over China has been better achieved with economic incentives and disincentives and international pressure than with unilateral U.S. pressure. The use of these measures within the military-to-military context appears inappropriate, however. Thus, a look at the evidence from several cases suggests that the U.S. military has very little influence over the PLA and the Chinese government. China is more influenced by international opinion than by U.S. pressure alone; economic incentives and disincentives have had a measured success in changing Chinese behavior; and the military relationship does not exist in a vacuum, but instead is primarily shaped by the tenor and atmosphere of the overall political and diplomatic relationship. (See pages 47–55.)

Reciprocity and Transparency

The most contentious issue is that of reciprocity and transparency. Chinese officials have long resisted efforts at greater transparency, arguing that "transparency is a tool of the strong to be used against the weak." For its part, the United States can be said to want transparency at the operational level whereas China wants transparency at the strategic level. Thus, until China is comfortable with U.S. strategic intentions, significant obstacles to reciprocity will continue to exist. While all interlocutors agree that there is a gap in transparency between the U.S. military and the PLA, there is disagreement over its degree and significance. Analysis of military exchanges indicates that the discrepancy over reciprocity and transparency does not revolve around the types of bases visited and the frequency of visits; rather it revolves around the U.S. military not being shown operational training or realistic exercises, to which the PLA has had access, and to the content of functional[1] visits. In addition, inefficiencies in the U.S. Defense Department's handling of its military relations with the PLA—inefficiencies in planning, conducting, and debriefing—have

---

[1] Functional refers to facility visits, student exchanges, and discussions of professional military topics. Activities are usually conducted between mid-level officers and officials.

limited the U.S. military's ability to properly exploit PLA transparency when it exists. (See pages 55–57.)

Overall Assessment and Policy Recommendations

Despite the problems encountered with carrying out the U.S.-China military relationship, there is value in continuing these activities. Although limitations in transparency and influence exist, the possibility of armed conflict between the United States and China warrants that a relationship be maintained to resolve differences and avoid misperceptions. This analysis recommends a three-part program of communication, information gathering, and limited cooperation. Communication can be conducted at the highest levels to signal strategic intent, clarify policy, and attempt to dissuade and deter China from taking actions inimical to U.S. interests. The relationship can also be used to gather information on the PLA to improve the U.S. military's understanding of PLA operations, doctrine, and role in the Chinese government. Finally, limited cooperation can take place when U.S. interests are at stake. Cooperation in the war against terror may be one prime example. Functional exchanges, however, like those conducted in the past to improve understanding will probably fail because of the lack of trust engendered by disagreements over strategic intent. (See pages 90–99.)

Acknowledgments

The author would like to thank the many people who were generous in freely giving their time to discuss U.S.-China military relations. They all provided valuable information and insights into the relationship. Because of the highly politicized nature of the issue, all prefer to remain nameless.

The author thanks James Mulvenon for his guidance in organizing the report, David Adamson, Eric Valko, and Jeanne Heller for their excellent editing of an early draft, and Heather Roy for valuable administrative support throughout the endeavor. He also thanks reviewers Roger Cliff and David Finkelstein for their comments and Jonathan Pollack and William Rosenau for their comments on an early version of this paper that will appear as a chapter in a larger volume on U.S. security cooperation in Asia.

Acronyms

ABM	Anti-Ballistic Missile (Treaty)
BWC	Biological Weapons Convention
CINCPAC	Commander-in-Charge, Pacific
CNA	Center for Naval Analyses
COCOM	Coordinating Committee for Multilateral Export Controls
CTBC	Comprehensive Test Ban Treaty
CWC	Chemical Weapons Convention
DCT	Defense Consultative Talks
ETIM	East Turkestan Islamic Movement
FPE	Functional and Professional Exchanges
GWOT	Global War On Terrorism
IPR	Intellectual Property Rights

IRBM	Intermediate Range Ballistic Missile
MMCA	Military Maritime Consultative Agreement
MTCR	Missile Technology Control Regime
NDAA	National Defense Authorization Act
NDU	National Defense University
NPR	Nuclear Posture Review
NPT	Nuclear Nonproliferation Treaty
OSD	Office of the Secretary of Defense
PLA	People's Liberation Army
PRC	People's Republic of China
PRM	Presidential Review Memorandum
QDR	Quadrennial Defense Review
RMA	Revolution in Military Affairs
SALT	Strategic Arms Limitation Treaty
SSGN	Guided Missile Nuclear Submarine
USCINCPAC	United States Commander in Charge, Pacific
WTO	World Trade Organization

CHAPTER ONE

Introduction

This report addresses the debate concerning U.S.-China military relations. Specifically, it examines the goals of U.S. policy, assesses the benefits of the current relationship, and proposes a revised policy based on a realistic assessment of what such a relationship can accomplish. It also reviews the history of U.S.-China military relations, particularly the transition from cooperation in support of a strategic rationale to cooperation to form a strategic rationale, and recommends a future military relations program based on U.S. and Chinese goals and the constraints placed on military-to-military activities by both sides.

The report argues that the fundamental reason for the instability in military-to-military ties with the People's Liberation Army (PLA) has been the pursuit of specific policies by each government that are perceived by each to be inimical to its respective interests. The relationship has thus been affected by the stances of the two countries over Taiwan and differences in overall strategic intent.

The distrust engendered by the pursuit of these policies has resulted in each side viewing the other as a potential enemy. Because of the potential for armed conflict between the United States and China, and because China is the weaker power, the PLA has been reluctant to share even the most basic information with the U.S. military in a belief that it has more to lose than the United States by being open. Thus, the PLA has been a reluctant partner in many activities with the U.S. Defense Department, resulting in limited benefits to the United States.

However, bureaucratic inefficiencies within the U.S. Defense Department have also limited the benefits of military-to-military activities with the PLA. Uncoordinated planning, execution, and debriefing as well as a lack of qualified China analysts directly leveraging access to the PLA have hindered the U.S. Defense Department's ability to identify, exploit, and assess the information it has gathered from its relationship with the PLA.

While the perceived lack of tangible benefits has led many observers to question whether the United States should have a military relationship with China, the sometimes contentious nature of U.S.-China relations and the possibility of armed conflict with China over Taiwan warrants that lines of communication should remain open to avoid misunderstandings and resolve misperceptions. Consequently, what in the past consisted of efforts to engage in security cooperation with China should now be better described as "security management." Such a program would consist of activities to manage the relationship so that it can prevent conflict, while taking into account the constraints and limitations present in the relationship. Specifically, this report recommends curtailing functional activities,[1] long complicated by disagreements over reciprocity and transparency, and instead focusing on high-level dialogue that will enable both sides to communicate policy and concerns and resolve misperceptions. In addition, it recommends that the U.S. Defense Department appoint a person (either civilian or military) with sufficient rank to reform the internal processes that it uses to manage military-to-military activities with the PLA.

The next chapter reviews the historical context of U.S.-China security cooperation from 1971 to the present and offers a short analysis of the difficulties inherent in the relationship. The chapter posits that the main issues dividing China and the United States have not been resolved and still affect the relationship today.

---

[1] Functional refers to facility visits, student exchanges, and discussions of professional military topics. Activities are usually conducted between mid-level officers and officials.

Chapter Three examines the current security environment between the United States and China and its implications for military-to-military relations. It concludes that there are numerous issues that hinder the development of a healthy relationship between the United States and China, but that these issues do not obviate the value of continuing contacts.

Chapter Four explores the debate surrounding military relations with the PLA and assesses the validity of the arguments. It observes that the PLA has been less open and has permitted less access to its facilities than has the U.S. military and concludes that to a limited extent Washington has been harmed by its military relationship with Beijing, whereas China has benefited somewhat from its military relationship with the United States.

Chapter Five examines PLA attitudes toward military relations with the United States. It reveals that the U.S. military and the PLA conduct relationships in fundamentally different ways. The PLA prefers a top-down approach, in which prior understanding of strategic issues can be operationalized at lower levels. The U.S. military, on the other hand, prefers a bottom-up approach that emphasizes identifying areas of cooperation through the implementation of activities at the working level. This fundamental difference has led the United States to propose activities that have not been fully supported by the PLA.

Chapter Six sets out the constraints imposed on the relationship by both the United States and China, assesses their impact on military-to-military activities, proposes a set of goals for these activities, and then recommends a course of action.

CHAPTER TWO

Historical Context

Although official military-to-military relations between the United States and the People's Republic of China (PRC) did not begin until Secretary of Defense Harold Brown's trip to Beijing in 1980, security cooperation between the United States and China was initiated from the outset of rapprochement in 1971, when Henry Kissinger shared intelligence on the Soviet military with his Chinese interlocutors. Since then, the relationship has developed in fits and starts as each side tried to determine a rationale for cooperating with the other. Throughout the more than 30 years of official and unofficial relations, differing strategic intent has played a role in hindering the relationship, but contention over Taiwan has been the most significant obstacle in furthering security cooperation, causing a deep level of distrust between the two sides and leading each to regard the other as a potential enemy.

Nixon and Ford Administrations

After the initial euphoria of President Richard Nixon's visit to China in 1972, U.S.-China relations, including military relations, developed slowly during the Nixon administration, mainly due to the Watergate scandal. Military cooperation at this early stage mainly consisted of "American statements of support for Chinese security against a Soviet attack and Chinese cooperation with American regional policy toward Korea, Japan, and Indochina."[1] During the Ford administration, the development of security cooperation with China was hindered by divisions within the administration over U.S. Soviet policy. Many in the U.S. government, especially in the State Department, feared that fostering military ties with China would antagonize the Soviet Union and could potentially ruin the spirit of détente. Consequently, the United States decided not to sell arms to China and not to endorse arms sales to China by U.S. allies. For their part, the Chinese also decided not to pursue enhanced security ties because of Washington's continued official recognition of Taiwan. They preferred instead to wait for formal U.S. recognition before expanding military ties.[2] The United States did make two exceptions to this policy. It approved the sale of two advanced computers with potential military applications to China's petroleum industry;[3] and in 1975 the United States protested, but did not block, a $200 million British sale of military jet engines.[4] These two sales notwithstanding, the overall bilateral relationship continued to flounder as neither side could define a strategic rationale sufficient to sustain relations,[5] "nor could the two sides assent to a formula for defusing the sensitive Taiwan question. As a result, the atmosphere of U.S.-Chinese ties was one of stagnation, if not outright deterioration."[6]

---

[1] Harry Harding, *A Fragile Relationship: The United States and China Since 1972*, Washington, D.C.: The Brookings Institute, 1992, p. 88. Specific areas of Chinese cooperation with the United States included ceasing criticism of the U.S.-Japan mutual security treaty, explicit support of peace and stability on the Korean peninsula, and support for a Cambodian government headed by King Norodom Sihanouk.

[2] Harding, p. 88.

[3] "Big-Computer Sale to Soviet Is Barred," *New York Times*, June 24, 1977, p. A3.

[4] George Lardner, Jr. and Jeffrey Smith, "Intelligence Ties Endure Despite U.S.-China Strain; 'Investment' Is Substantial, Longstanding," *Washington Post*, June 25, 1989, p. A1.

[5] Thanks to Roger Cliff for this point.

[6] Jonathan Pollack, *The Lessons of Coalition Politics: Sino-American Security Relations*, Santa Monica: RAND Corporation, 1984, p. 25.

Carter Administration

When the Carter administration took office in 1977, it began a review of U.S.-China policy that, in part, reevaluated U.S. policies toward the sale of defense-related technology and equipment to China.[7] The assessment, entitled Presidential Review Memorandum (PRM)-24, concluded that if the United States sold military technology to China,

> Moscow would then be compelled to make a fundamental reassessment of its policies toward the U.S. . . . Soviet perceptions of the threat of U.S.-Chinese military collaboration would stiffen Soviet positions on even the major issues of U.S.-Soviet relations such as SALT . . . The Soviets might also increase tensions with China.[8]

Based on this assessment, President Jimmy Carter decided against weapon sales to China. In May 1978, however, he did send national security adviser Zbigniew Brzezinski to China to discuss normalization and to signal displeasure with Soviet expansionism.[9] Brzezinski announced that "the significance of the trip was to underline the long-term strategic nature of the United States relationship to China."[10] During these meetings the two sides discussed U.S.-Soviet arms talks and the global security environment. The United States also shared military intelligence with China and proposed an exchange of visits by military delegations.[11] During these meetings the United States informed the Chinese that it would not object to sales

---

[7] "Presidential Review memorandum/NSC 24," http://www.jimmycarterlibrary.org/documents/prmemorandums/prm24.pdf.

[8] Bernard Weinraub, "U.S. Study Sees Peril in Selling Arms to China," *New York Times*, June 24, 1977, pp. A1, A3.

[9] Harding, p. 88.

[10] Bernard Gwertzman, "Brzezinski Gave Details to China on Arms Talks with Soviet Union," *New York Times*, May 28, 1978, p. 1.

[11] Zbigniew Brzezinski, *Power and Principle: Memoirs of the National Security Adviser 1977–1981*, New York: Farrar, Straus, Giroux, 1983, p. 209.

to China of defensive arms by such countries as France and Britain and would permit the sale of U.S. dual-use technology.[12]

After normalization in 1979, the prospect for further security cooperation appeared to be improving. In a *Time* interview, Deng Xiaoping stated, "If we really want to be able to place curbs on the polar bear, the only realistic thing for us is to unite. If we only depend on the strength of the United States, it is not enough."[13] Deng seemed ready to back up his words with action. During meetings with the administration, Deng informed President Carter that China would attack Vietnam to punish it for a host of provocations, including its closeness with the Soviet Union and invasion of Cambodia. Deng's apparent attempt to elicit U.S. rhetorical support for the invasion, however, met a tepid response. After returning to China, Deng discussed expanding the security relationship with a Senate Foreign Relations Committee delegation and proposed "port calls by the American Navy, Chinese purchases of American arms and the establishment of American monitoring facilities on Chinese soil to verify Moscow's compliance with Soviet-American arms control agreements."[14] This last offer was in fact initiated by the Carter administration during Deng's visit to the United States in 1979.[15] These latter proposals were cautiously received by the United States. When Brzezinski followed up on Deng's proposals with Ambassador Chai Zemin, Chai informed Brzezinski that, in protest of the Taiwan Relations Act (TRA),[16] China was not willing to conduct more exten-

---

[12] Bernard Gwerztman, "U.S. Reported Acting to Strengthen Ties with Peking Regime," *New York Times*, June 26, 1978, pp. 1, 7.

[13] "An Interview with Teng Hsiao-p'ing," *Time*, February 5, 1979, p. 34.

[14] Harding, p. 90.

[15] Patrick Tyler, *A Great Wall: Six Presidents and China*, New York: The Century Foundation, 1999, pp. 277–278.

[16] The Taiwan Relations Act passed on April 10, 1979 committed U.S. policy to providing Taiwan with arms of a defensive character and maintaining the ability of the United States to resist any resort to force or other forms of coercion that would jeopardize the security, or the social or economic system, of the people on Taiwan.

sive military-to-military activities, although the cool U.S. response to China's invasion of Vietnam may also have been a factor.[17]

The Soviet invasion of Afghanistan in late 1979 forced a reassessment of U.S. China policy, resulting in a decision to pursue a more extensive security relationship with Beijing. Nevertheless, President Carter decided not to sell weapons to China, saying that "it would be a quantum leap to go to arms sales" at that time, although he did decide that the United States would be willing to sell an over-the-horizon radar to China.[18] Later in the year, however, the United States expressed its willingness to sell nonlethal military equipment to China, including a ground station to receive data from Landsat satellites, transport aircraft, military helicopters, and communications equipment, with the sale of lethal military equipment to be approved on a case-by-case basis.[19] It was also reported that the Chinese agreed to accelerate shipments of arms and equipment to the Afghan rebels.[20]

Defense Secretary Harold Brown described U.S.-China security cooperation during this time as having

> proceeded during the 1970s from enmity through conversations and normalization to friendship and potential partnership [including] a mutual examination of the global strategic situation . . . exchanging views on the balance of forces in various parts of the world, indicating to each other what our own intentions are, [and] what our own plans are. Not planning together, but mentioning to the other what our programs and plans are.[21]

This new opening also resulted in a series of high-level exchanges and other activities. General Geng Biao and Deputy Chief of the General Staff Liu Huaqing visited the United States in 1980.

---

[17] Harding, p. 91.

[18] Brzezinski, p. 431.

[19] Harding, p. 92.

[20] Lardner and Smith, p. A1.

[21] Defense Secretary Harold Brown, Interview on ABC News "Issues and Answers," January 13, 1980, quoted in Pollack, p. 14.

Following that, Under Secretary of Defense for Research and Engineering William Perry visited Beijing in September 1980, where he informed the Chinese that the U.S. government "had approved more than 400 export licenses for various dual-use items and military support equipment. These included items as disparate as geophysical computers, heavy trucks, C-130 transports, and Chinook helicopters."[22] In April, Washington removed China from the same Coordinating Committee for Multilateral Export Controls (COCOM)[23] category as the Warsaw Pact (category Y) and placed China in its own classification (category P), "making China eligible for a wider variety of exports, particularly in such sensitive areas as transport aircraft, long-distance communications equipment, and military-type helicopters."[24]

Whereas the normalization of relations in 1979 led to the development of full state-to-state relations, including the posting of attachés and officer exchanges, the sale of military equipment and dual-use technology continued to prove problematic for U.S. officials. One dilemma was defining the purpose of the sales in regard to the Soviets. Was the United States interested in modernizing the PLA primarily to make it more effective against the Soviet military or should the mere *prospect* of military sales to China be used to deter Soviet actions? If military sales were to proceed without Soviet provocation, the sales would lose their deterrent value. The United States also recognized that arms sales to China raised concerns among allies and friends, especially considering that China refused to give firm commitments not to transfer technology to third parties.[25]

The Chinese, on the other hand, were confronted with significant internal problems. Reductions of almost 25 percent in the de-

---

[22] Pollack, p. 70.

[23] COCOM was founded in 1950 to stop the export of military and dual-use technology to Warsaw Pact countries. It was later expanded to include China, Mongolia, and Laos. In 1995 it was replaced by the Wassenaar Arrangement on Export Controls for Conventional Arms and Dual-use Goods and Technologies.

[24] Brzezinski, p. 424.

[25] Pollack, pp. 19–20.

fense budget in the late 1970s made it increasingly unlikely that the PLA would have been able to afford U.S. military equipment, even if the United States had offered it. In addition, Chinese industry was unprepared both technologically and organizationally to absorb large infusions of high technology.[26] But China, like the United States, also valued arms sales for their political significance. To China, the U.S. refusal to expand military sales demonstrated that the United States did not take its relations with China seriously.[27] Consequently, despite U.S. offerings in 1980, expanded U.S.-China military ties continued to prove elusive.

Reagan Administration

In 1981 the Reagan administration came into office with doubts about the value of relations with China, especially in regard to Taiwan. Although export licenses for nontechnical goods were being approved, licenses for technology transfers were being vetoed by the Defense Department. More important, the United States announced that it would sell a package of military spare parts to Taiwan.[28] Consequently, U.S.-China relations for the last part of 1981 and much of 1982 were stalled over the issue of arms sales to Taiwan. This in turn affected defense technology transfers and geopolitics. Arms sales to Taiwan was the most important issue and the one on which China tended to base its U.S. policy. According to Beijing, a lack of agreement on this matter would impede progress on other issues. Defense technology transfer was connected to the Taiwan question in that China did not want to give the impression that the United States could buy China's acquiescence to arms sales to the island. Thus, there could be no movement on arms sales until the Taiwan arms sales question was resolved. China also threatened that a failure on

---

[26] Pollack, pp. 20–21.

[27] Pollack, p. 17.

[28] Tyler, pp. 317–319.

the part of the United States to reach an agreement on the arms sales issue would affect other areas of U.S.-China cooperation.[29]

The signing of the U.S.-PRC Joint Communiqué on August 17, 1982, in which the United States stated that it "intends to reduce gradually its sales of arms to Taiwan, leading over a period of time to a final resolution," temporarily ended the disagreement over arms sales to Taiwan. In May of the following year, policy debates within the Reagan administration led to a presidential decision to switch China's COCOM status from category P to the less restrictive category V, which also governed arms sales to West European nations, India, most of Africa, some Arab countries, Australia, New Zealand, and Japan.[30]

The military relationship was put on a better footing when in September 1983 Secretary of Defense Caspar Weinberger proposed in Beijing what came to be known as the "three pillars" approach to military relations with China: high-level visits, functional-level exchanges, and military technology cooperation. The two sides agreed in principle to resume military ties, including exchanges on training, logistics, and military tactics.[31]

The reaction to the new policy within the Pentagon was mixed. At this time there were still many senior U.S. military officers on active duty who had fought in Korea against the Chinese or who had been posted on assignments where China was viewed as the enemy. In addition, some feared that any interaction with China would be at the expense of Taiwan.[32] Despite these concerns, the three pillars policy was carried out and military relations with China developed steadily. In 1984 the Chinese agreed to sell portable surface-to-air missiles to the Contra rebels in Nicaragua.[33] In 1986 the U.S. Navy made a port call to Qingdao and the U.S. Air Force Thunderbirds

---

[29] Pollack, pp. 90–92.

[30] Pollack, p. 108.

[31] Pollack, p. 118.

[32] Interview.

[33] Oliver North, *Under Fire: An American Story*, New York: Harper Collins, 1991, p. 258.

performed in Beijing the following year. By 1987 four weapon technology transfers had been signed: a $22 million large-caliber artillery plant modernization program, an $8 million MK-46 Mod 2 torpedo sale, a $62 million AN/TPQ-37 artillery-locating radar sale, and a $500 million F-8 interceptor avionics modernization program (Peace Pearl).[34] These technologies were chosen to increase China's capability against the Soviet Union and were in some cases modified to pose less of a threat to Taiwan or the United States. In addition to these programs were a variety of functional exchanges carried out by the Army, Navy, and Air Force.[35]

While the PLA was gaining hardware from these exchanges, the U.S. military was gaining a better picture of the PLA through both the number and quality of contacts. In response to the PLA's reluctance to reveal motivations for wanting certain technologies, U.S. military negotiators argued that in order to provide the most suitable equipment to China they needed to know PLA operational and technical requirements. The U.S. methodology would also lead to a better understanding of the Chinese military, but the Chinese were not interested in giving anything away. Beijing sought to limit the scope of the defense relationship to defense technology transfer only, whereas the United States viewed this cooperation as but one of three pillars to be pursued. Yet the Chinese also understood that, to receive technological cooperation, they would ultimately have to cooperate with the United States in the other two areas.

In 1987, however, irritants in the overall relationship once again interfered with the progression of military ties. U.S. concerns over Chinese sales of Silkworm antiship missiles to Iran caused many in the Defense Department to reevaluate military ties with China, especially after China publicly denied that such sales ever took place. Many felt that these missiles would be used against the U.S. Navy in

---

[34] Eden Y. Woon, "Chinese Arms Sales and U.S.-China Military Relations," *Asian Survey*, Vol. XXIX, No. 6, June 1989, p. 602.

[35] Thomas L. Wilborn, "Security Cooperation with China: Analysis and a Proposal," *U.S. Army War College*, November 25, 1994, http://carlisle-www.army.mil/usassi/ssipubs/pubs94/coopchna/coopchna.pdf.

the Persian Gulf. In October 1987, the "State Department announced a decision to suspend additional liberalization of high-technology transfers to China, stating that because of 'rising tensions in the Persian Gulf . . . we consider this an inappropriate time to proceed with our review of further export control liberalization.'"[36] The suspension was lifted in March 1988 after China agreed to stop delivery of Silkworm missiles to Iran, but hopes of enhancing defense ties were again put in doubt when it was revealed that China sold CSS-2 Intermediate Range Ballistic Missiles (IRBMs) to Saudi Arabia.[37] To many in the United States, the CSS-2 sale coupled with the Silkworm sales to Iran proved that "Chinese arms sales policy was in conflict with U.S. interests."[38]

George H. W. Bush and Clinton Administrations

The Tiananmen massacre on June 4, 1989 deeply affected Sino-U.S. relations for most of the Bush administration. The United States suspended all military-to-military activities with the PLA, including regular attaché activities, arms sales, technology transfer agreements, and functional and high-level exchanges. In the early 1990s, however, the United States began to reassess its military relationship with China, resulting in an easing of some of the post-Tiananmen restrictions. In December 1992, for example, the Bush administration approved the release of four antisubmarine torpedoes, two artillery-locating radars, equipment for a munitions-production line, and electronics gear to upgrade F-8 aircraft purchased by China before the Tiananmen massacre.[39]

---

[36] Woon, p. 612.

[37] Woon, p. 613.

[38] Woon, p. 613.

[39] Keith Bradsher, "U.S. Will Release Weapons to China," *New York Times,* December 23, 1992, p. A12.

During this time, a diverse group of politicians and experts began arguing that having no relations was preventing the United States from learning about and influencing the PLA. Representative Patricia Schroeder stated that ending the ban on military contacts "is not for their good, it's for our good, if we can be blunt about it. . . . We've had a terrific problem with [China] selling weapons to countries we don't like, like Iraq. We'd like to know what their intentions are, which way their guns are pointed, whether they have their own agenda. These are things we don't pick up through satellites." China scholar Paul Godwin also argued that "the suspension of high-level military contacts is hurting us in the long run. If we want to talk to the Chinese about problems of nonproliferation, we've got to talk to the military."[40] Even Representative Nancy Pelosi, a long-time critic of China, stated that "there is no problem [with engagement] as long as we continue to put pressure on China where it's needed."[41]

In mid-September 1993, President Bill Clinton reportedly signed an action memorandum that authorized the U.S. government to conduct a broad engagement plan with China. This was followed in July 1994 by a memo by Secretary of Defense William Perry that explained his views on relations with the PLA and stated the rationale for expanding military relations:

> China is fast becoming the world's largest economic power, and that combined with its UN PermFive status, its political clout, its nuclear weapons and a modernizing military, make China a player with which the United States must work together. Our security posture dramatically improves if China cooperates with us. In order to regain that cooperation, we must rebuild mutual trust and understanding with the PLA, and this could only happen through high-level dialogue and working level contacts. I should note that arms sales are not contemplated at this time,

---

[40] Jim Mann, "Administration Urged to Renew China Defense Ties; Diplomacy: U.S. Needs Military Contacts to Keep Abreast of Beijing's Arms Sales, Buildups, Officials Say," *Los Angeles Times*, March 7, 1993, p. A1.

[41] Daniel Williams and R. Jeffrey Smith, "U.S. to Renew Contact with Chinese Military; Meeting Reflects Strategy of Easing Tension," *Washington Post*, November 1, 1993, p. A1.

and we will raise human rights concerns even in high-level military discussions. . . .

The military relationship with China could pay significant dividends for DoD. Let us proceed in a forward-looking, although measured, manner in this important relationship.[42]

Perry further elaborated his rationale for military relations with China in a speech to the Washington State China Relations Council, stating that he believed that engagement with China would provide opportunities to the United States to influence China's policies on regional issues and to help curb the spread of weapons of mass destruction. He also asserted that engagement could make the PLA more open and lessen the chances of misunderstandings.[43] Perry later made an October 1994 four-day trip to China. During meetings the two sides discussed human rights and signed an accord to create a Joint Defense Conversion Commission to better enable Chinese military plants to produce civilian products.[44] This commission focused on projects involved in modernizing China's air traffic control system and developing electric cars.[45]

Some criticized the Clinton administration's new overall "comprehensive engagement plan" for its inconsistency. Critics pointed out, for example, that the State Department would complain about Beijing's human rights abuses while the Defense Department conducted meetings with military officers who were involved in the Tiananmen massacre. These types of mixed signals may have led

---

[42] Secretary of Defense William Perry, Memorandum for the Secretaries of the Army, Navy, and Air Force Concerning the U.S.-China Military Relationship, July 1994, http://www.gwu.edu/~nsaarchiv/NSAEBB/NSAEBB19/12-01.htm.

[43] "U.S. Strategy: Engage China, Not Contain It," remarks delivered by Secretary of Defense William H. Perry to the Washington State China Relations Council, October 30, 1995.

[44] Steven Mufson, "U.S. to Help China Retool Arms Plants; Perry Received as 'Old Friend' in Quest of Military Ties; Human Rights Discussed," *Washington Post,* October 18, 1994, p. A28.

[45] U.S. Department of Defense, DoD News Briefing, January 18, 1996, www.defenselink.mil.

China to become confused over the priorities of the United States' engagement policy. China specialist Harry Harding stated, "We decided to talk to China before we were clear about what we had to say. As a result, it's very easy for the Chinese to misunderstand what the United States is about."[46]

During this time, critics of U.S.-China military ties no longer focused on the U.S. Soviet policy but on human rights and Taiwan. After a controversial Chinese delegation visit to the United States, human rights activist Drew Liu asserted:

> the administration should look at the bigger picture and push for a change from communism to constitutional democracy. . . . If that is not made clear, it will send the wrong signal to the Chinese military that it's OK to kill and suppress democratic activists and students, and we'll do business even if there is blood on their hands, and that's wrong.[47]

Others argued that continuing military contacts would enable the Chinese to acquire U.S. military technology, pointing out that assisting China's military industry to convert to civilian production would increase profits to the PLA and make it easier for the PLA to purchase modern equipment. These concerns led Congress to pass a law in 1995 that barred the Pentagon from assisting the PLA with defense conversion. One aide described Congress as "deeply suspicious of the entire U.S.-communist China military-to-military program" and the defense conversion program as "basically a siphon pump from U.S. defense contractors to the Chinese defense establishment."[48]

Still, military relations continued apace through the summer of 1995, until the United States granted a visa to Taiwan president Lee

---

[46] Daniel Williams, "China Finds 'Comprehensive Engagement' Hard to Grasp," *Washington Post*, February 13, 1995, p. A17.

[47] Bill Gertz, "China's New Era at Pentagon; 'Red Carpet' Rolled Out to General Tainted by Massacre," *Washington Times*, August 18, 1994, p. A3.

[48] Bill Gertz, "Panel Clips Perry's Wings, Bars Links to China's Military," *Washington Times*, May 29, 1995, p. A4.

Teng-hui to allow him to make a speech at his alma mater, Cornell University. China responded to Lee's visit by canceling the visit of Defense Minister General Chi Haotian to Washington and firing missiles into areas around Taiwan in the summer of 1995. Interestingly, military relations were not immediately harmed by these 1995 missile operations. In fact, high-level U.S. visits continued. In September and November, respectively, president of the National Defense University Lieutenant General Ervin Rokke and Assistant Secretary of Defense Joseph Nye visited China. In addition, General Chi was reinvited to travel to the United States in the spring of 1996.

The development of military relations was slowed more significantly in March 1996 when the PLA conducted another round of missile operations to influence Taiwan's first democratic presidential election. In response, the United States cancelled the visit of General Chi scheduled for April. Yet while China's missile operations caused a rethinking of overall China policy in the Clinton administration, the National Security Council in the spring of 1996 finished a review of China policy that concluded that the administration would focus on "the big picture." With that, the administration decided to repair ties with China by again focusing on "comprehensive engagement." According to one White House official:

> The overall strategy was that no one agency run off on its own. No freelancing on sanctions events or other things that would have a profound effect on relations. This was not a decision to suck up or appease. It was a decision to consider consequences rather than automatically heading to a solution that would satisfy a vocal domestic audience.[49]

In December 1996, General Chi made the trip to the United States that had been cancelled in March. During this trip China agreed "in principle" to continue to allow U.S. warships to conduct port calls in Hong Kong. The two sides also agreed to exchange ship visits. The Chinese Navy would visit Hawaii and the West Coast in

---

[49] Barton Gellman, "Reappraisal Led to New China Policy; Skeptics Abound, But U.S. 'Strategic Partnership' Yielding Results," *Washington Post*, June 22, 1998, p. A1.

the spring of 1997, followed by a U.S. Navy visit to China. Chi's trip, however, was protested on human rights grounds. Representative Nancy Pelosi stated, "I hope that our Secretary of Defense would not give full military honors to the person who was in operational control of the troops in Tiananmen Square and who directed the military action to intimidate the people of Taiwan at the time of their presidential election."[50]

For the Clinton administration, by contrast, the 1996 missile operations gave further credence to the need for military relations with China and, in 1997 and 1998, both sides agreed to restore the number of functional and professional exchanges, high-level visits, multilateral dialogues and confidence-building measures. The U.S. desire to expand ties with the PLA was evident in General John Shalikashvili's May 1997 speech to the PLA's National Defense University in which he stated:

> For our part, to accomplish these objectives, the United States wants: a more equal exchange of information with the PLA; the development of confidence building measures to reduce further the possibility of miscalculations; military academic and functional exchanges; PLA participation in multinational military activities; and a regular dialogue between our senior military leaderships.[51]

In October 1997, President Clinton hosted Chinese President Jiang Zemin in Washington, D.C. The visit resulted in an agreement on conducting military maritime safety consultations and on information sharing for humanitarian crises and disaster relief.[52] In December 1997, the United States and China held their first Defense Consultative Talks (DCT) between Lieutenant General Xiong

---

[50] Bill Gertz, "Chinese Generals Visits Draws Fire; Pelosi Rips Honors for Tiananmen Massacre Architect," *Washington Times*, November 26, 1996, p. A8.

[51] John M. Shalikashvili, "Remarks to PLA National Defense University on U.S.-China Engagement: The Role of Military-to-Military Contacts, May 14, 1997, www.defenselink.mil.

[52] White House, "Fact Sheet: Accomplishments of U.S.-China Summit," October 29, 1997.

Guangkai and Under Secretary of Defense for Policy Walter Slo-combe.[53] During these meetings both sides briefed each other on humanitarian relief missions and search-and-rescue operations. Pentagon spokesman Kenneth Bacon described the talks as being

> designed to increase understanding, to increase transparency. They're based on the very simple premise that the world's most powerful nation and the world's most populous nation have to be able to deal with each other in an adult, mature way both in areas where they agree and areas where they disagree.[54]

The robust military relationship continued into 1998. In the beginning of 1998, reports surfaced that Secretary of Defense William Cohen was advocating the sale of spare parts for the 24 Black Hawk helicopters that were sold to China in 1984. The Chinese claimed to be unable to operate the Black Hawks due to the lack of spare parts, and the unwillingness of the United States to transfer the spares had been a point of contention for China in its relations with the U.S. military. In response to a question about the sale of the parts, Cohen replied that he

> would hope that there would be progress made on issues that are of concern to the Congress of the United States and to President Clinton in the field of human rights. Assuming progress is made, I'm sure that we can also make progress dealing with the removal of certain sanctions.[55]

Secretary Cohen traveled to Beijing in January 1998, where he signed the Military Maritime Consultative Agreement (MMCA), an agreement designed to reduce the chances of confrontation between

---

[53] In December 1994, Ted Warner, Assistant Secretary for Strategy and Requirements, went to China to brief the PLA on the U.S. military's plans, budget, and the six-year defense plan. It was not officially called a Defense Consultative Talk.

[54] John Pomfret, "Pentagon Talks May Lead to More U.S.-China Military Cooperation, Joint Exercises," *Washington Post,* December 12, 1997, p. A12.

[55] U.S. Department of Defense, DoD News Briefing, January 20, 1998, www.defenselink. mil.

the two militaries in the air and on the sea. Secretary Cohen also visited a facility described by the Chinese as the Beijing Military Region Air Force Command Center, charged with monitoring air and missile defenses for 200 miles around Beijing. This tour, the first of its kind, was described by Cohen as a very important, but symbolic step by the Chinese to "start sharing more information, to start conducting more exchanges and visits."[56] Cohen also stated that the United States wanted to deepen the relationship, but that he was "not seeking to rush or accelerate this change in our relationship." Despite this, Cohen went on to say that the two sides did discuss cooperation on humanitarian missions, which would have been a significant upgrade in U.S.-China military relations.[57] Still, China continued to restrict certain areas of engagement. Requests by the U.S. Air Force Chief of Staff to fly a Chinese Su-27 fighter jet were denied and the Chinese responded that they would "study" a request for the two sides to visit each other's nuclear weapons sites.[58]

Despite these continuing obstacles, however, military relations at the end of the 1990s were undeniably at their most robust since the end of the 1980s. By 1999, the United States military had visited numerous PLA facilities and bases, including several logistics units, PLA Navy bases, and military academies. There was also an increase in the number of visits to the United States by members of the PLA. A PLA delegation had visited Fort Hood, Texas and flown over a mile-long formation of M1A1 tanks. PLA members had made arrested landings on an aircraft carrier and visited aircraft carriers in port. U.S. military officers, taking the cue from higher-level defense officials, proceeded ahead with a more robust program than some

---

[56] The alleged Beijing Military Region Air Force Command Center in question is suspected by many to have been a fake.

[57] U.S. Deparment of Defense, January 20, 1998.

[58] John Pomfret, "Cohen Hails Achievements in China Visit; Halt in Missile Sales to Iran, Closer Military Ties Cited," *Washington Post*, January 20, 1998, p. A11. Contractual obligations to the Russians also played a role in the Su-27 denial.

non-uniformed officials had ordered or would have liked, resulting in at least one instance of unauthorized access to a U.S. submarine.[59]

During the mid-1990s, military ties had grown to such a level that several interlocutors wondered if the program had gotten out of control. In 1998 and 1999, hearings on Chinese espionage against the United States held by the United States House of Representatives Select Committee on U.S. National Security and Military/Commercial Concerns with the People's Republic of China, otherwise known as the Cox Committee,[60] drew more attention to U.S.-China military relations and questioned the rationale for those ties. Congressional scrutiny focused specifically on the Pentagon's program with the PLA after the *Washington Times* leaked a Defense Department "game plan" calling for 80 military-to-military activities in 1999. These included "12 high-level visits by Pentagon and PLA officials, 40 functional exchanges of working-level military officials, 16 confidence-building measures and 13 international security meetings."[61] Included among the planned activities were PLA observation of training maneuvers by the 3rd Army, paratroop operations by the 82nd Airborne Division, briefings on logistics, and a trip to Sandia National Laboratory. In response to the article, Representative Dana Rohrabacher stated, "It's crazy to modernize a potential enemy's ability to fight a war, and that's what we're doing."[62] Representative Benjamin Gilman was also concerned with the planned exchanges. In a letter to Secretary Cohen, Gilman wrote:

> It is inconceivable to me that the administration is proceeding with these visits to our military facilities despite the recent revelations about Chinese espionage at our nuclear weapons labs. Accordingly, I am requesting the Pentagon to curtail these visits

---

[59] Interview.

[60] The Cox Committee was set up to investigate allegations of illegal transfers of dual-use and military technology to China.

[61] Bill Gertz, "Military Exchanges with Beijing Raises Security Concerns," *Washington Times*, February 19, 1999, p. A1.

[62] Gertz, p. A1.

at this time. The fundamental questions we should be asking
are: Are we enhancing Beijing's ability to resolve the future of
Taiwan by military means? Are we improving Beijing's capability to threaten U.S. interests in Asia?[63]

Senator Jesse Helms, also in a letter to Secretary Cohen, expressed his
misgivings about the planned activities, stating:

> I have grave concerns about the Department of Defense's
> "Game Plan for 1999 U.S.-Sino Defense Exchanges," because at
> its most fundamental level, the department's plan assumes that
> Communist China is a "strategic partner" worthy of participat-
> ing in a multitude of military exchanges and visits. . . . Red
> China is the same country that has just been caught in the theft
> of our nation's most vital nuclear secrets from a national weap-
> ons laboratory. No other incident of atomic espionage, includ-
> ing that of the Rosenbergs, has so deeply harmed our national
> security.[64]

A congressional aide also questioned the Pentagon's responsiveness to
these criticisms, asserting:

> We keep asking tough questions about the purpose and rationale
> for these visits, and all we get are vague answers. It's time Con-
> gress got its arms around this and consider legislation to con-
> strain such visits so that the Chinese military cannot benefit.[65]

The Pentagon's proposed plan for 1999 military activities with
China was unexpectedly halted in May 1999 when the United States
accidentally bombed the Chinese embassy in Belgrade. Beijing responded with vigorous diplomatic protests and U.S. diplomatic facilities were overwhelmed by popular protests. This suspension contin-

---

[63] Bill Gertz, "General Postpones Trip to China," *Washington Times*, March 22, 1999, p.
A1.

[64] Bill Gertz, "Helms Calls for Less Exchange with China," *Washington Times*, March 26,
1999, p. A4.

[65] Bill Gertz, "General Postpones China Trip," *Washington Times*, March 22, 1999, p. A1.

ued until October 31, when Beijing permitted a U.S. destroyer to visit Hong Kong, and was not officially lifted until Deputy Assistant Secretary of Defense for East Asia Kurt Campbell traveled to China in November to discuss restarting the relationship.

The congressional scrutiny that began in early 1999 continued into the fall and resulted in provisions in the 2000 National Defense Authorization Act (NDAA) forbidding any

> military-to-military exchange or contact that included inappropriate exposure to the PLA in the areas of force projection operations, nuclear operations, advanced logistical operations, chemical and biological defense and other capabilities related to weapons of mass destruction, surveillance and reconnaissance operations, joint warfighting experiments and other activities related to a transformation in warfare, military space operations, other advanced capabilities of the Armed Forces, arms sales or military-related technology transfers, release of classified or restricted information.[66]

In January 2000, PLA Lieutenant General Xiong Guangkai traveled to Washington to discuss the military-to-military plan for the year. According to one official, the talks were designed to result in a modest increase in activities "that acknowledges the delicacy of the environment, politically, and to take careful steps given what has transpired."[67] By July 2000, the relationship had been restored to the point that Secretary Cohen was able to travel to Beijing. During this time, Cohen stated that the United States and China were planning a sand table exercise on humanitarian assistance and revealed that ship visits would be carried out and a medical delegation would come to the United States. An environmental cooperation agreement was also signed.[68] The program for 2000, while not as extensive as those con-

---

[66] U.S. Department of Defense, *Report of Past Military to Military Exchanges and Contacts Between the U.S. and PRC*, undated.

[67] Steven Lee Myers, "Chinese Military to Resume Contacts With the Pentagon," *New York Times*, January 6, 2000, p A10.

[68] U.S. Department of Defense, Secretary of Defense William S. Cohen News Briefing, July 13, 2000, www.defenselink.mil.

ducted in the previous years, was still robust, with a total of 34 activities including four defense policy visits, six high-level visits, 11 professional visits, seven confidence-building measures, and six multinational fora.[69] But the new activities were not immune from congressional scrutiny. In August 2000, a delegation from the PLA Academy of Military Sciences visited the Joint Forces Command, a trip that drew the ire of Senator Robert Smith who stated that he was "shocked that DoD appears to be thwarting the law with regard to the Smith/Delay U.S.-PRC military-to-military restrictions."[70]

George W. Bush Administration

When the Bush administration entered office, Secretary of Defense Donald Rumsfeld began a review of all military contacts with China. In response to criticism of the previous administration's policies, Rumsfeld wanted a clearer picture of the Defense Department's overall program with the PLA so as to institute discipline into the management of military contacts and to enable the U.S. military to better respond to China's lack of reciprocity and transparency. Rumsfeld was reviewing the forthcoming scheduled activities on a monthly basis when the process came to a crashing halt after the collision of a Chinese fighter jet with a U.S. EP-3 electronic surveillance plane in April 2001. By May 2001, however, the policy was loosened when the Pentagon announced that it would approve all contacts with the PLA on a case-by-case basis. In September, a meeting was held under the Military Maritime Consultative Agreement on how to better avoid incidents such as the EP-3 collision. In December, the first port visit to Hong Kong since the collision took place as well as another meeting to discuss the MMCA. Activities have continued on a limited basis since the end of 2001, including National Defense Univer-

---

[69] Letter to Representative Bob Stump from Paul Wolfowitz on military-to-military exchanges with the People's Liberation Army, June 8, 2001.

[70] Bill Gertz, "Chinese Visit Sensitive Military Facilities," *Washington Times*, August 24, 2000, p. A1.

sity (NDU) and National War College visits, another meeting to discuss maritime safety, and an effort to search for the remains of two American pilots who were shot down over China while conducting a spy mission in 1952.

In response to the terrorist attacks on September 11, 2001, China offered to conduct search and rescue operations for pilots downed in its territory and moved troops to its border with Afghanistan to prevent border crossings, as well as taking a number of other nonmilitary measures. Direct military cooperation, however, apparently did not take place and appears not to have been seriously pursued by the U.S. military. U.S. Central Command commander General Tommy Franks has stated:

> We have not pursued basing or staging or overflight from my command with China, because, as you know, Afghanistan is a country surrounded by a lot of other countries, and each of them has been forthcoming in terms of movement of both humanitarian assistance and support as well as military support and military formations and forces in and out of Afghanistan.[71]

Some believe that Chinese behavior during the EP-3 crisis has hardened the attitudes of the Pentagon leadership against cooperation with China. Officially, however, the Pentagon remains open to military-to-military activities and has stated that the main factors on which a military relationship will be based are reciprocity and transparency.[72] Deputy Secretary of Defense Paul Wolfowitz has stated:

> contact between American military personnel and Chinese military personnel can reduce misunderstanding on both sides and can help build a better basis for co-operation when opportunities

---

[71] U.S. Department of Defense, General Tommy Franks Press Briefing, April 11, 2002, www.defenselink.mil.

[72] Michael R. Gordon, "Rumsfeld Limiting Military Contacts with the Chinese," *New York Times*, June 4, 2001, p. A1.

arise. So we'd like to enhance those opportunities for interaction. . . .[73]

In December 2002, Under Secretary Douglas Feith held the fifth round of Defense Consultative Talks with the PLA. During this meeting the PLA proposed a set of military-to-military activities with the U.S. military, which Feith stated would be studied. Reciprocity and transparency issues were also discussed, with no apparent conclusion.[74]

Conclusion

The development of U.S.-China military relations has historically been hindered by differing strategic calculations, and the challenges of harmonizing the strategic calculations of the two countries have prevented the establishment of a solid foundation for the military relationship. In the 1970s and 1980s, for example, the U.S. debate centered on each country's respective policies toward the Soviet Union, with the United States concerned that any commitment to China's security could lead to a more aggressive Soviet foreign policy and China concerned about the entanglements of a formal alliance and the implications of Sino-American rapprochement on potential reunification with Taiwan. During the 1990s, the original strategic rationale for the relationship—opposition to the Soviet Union—was no longer viable. Instead, military relations had changed from cooperation in support of a strategic rationale to cooperation to form a strategic rationale. It was thought that by engaging China, the United States could better ease China's entrance into the international community. Despite efforts to improve military relations, however, the Taiwan issue and mutual distrust of each other's strategic intentions

---

[73] U.S. Department of Defense, "Deputy Secretary Wolfowitz Interview with Phoenix Television," May 31, 2002, www.defenselink.mil.

[74] U.S. Department of Defense, "Under Secretary Feith Media Roundtable on U.S. China Defense Consultative Talks," December 9, 2002, www.defenselink.mil.

have continually hampered the relationship. Without a resolution of these issues, a fundamental improvement in the military relationship has remained elusive.

CHAPTER THREE

Strategic Factors Affecting U.S.-China Security Relations

The U.S.-China military relationship cannot be divorced from the overall bilateral relationship, so it is of interest to examine the current state of U.S.-China relations. Although bilateral ties were harmed by the EP-3 incident, U.S.-China relations have remained stable and have improved since its resolution. China and the United States have been able to cooperate in diplomatic, economic, and security areas. President Bush dropped his campaign description of China as a strategic competitor, asserting instead that "America wants a constructive relationship with China."[1] Beijing, for its part, has supported the United States in the war on terror and stated in February 2002 that the United States and China would "intensify high-level strategic dialogue, as well as contacts between various agencies" of the U.S. and PRC governments.[2]

Lurking behind this tactical improvement in relations, however, are irritants in the overall bilateral relationship. Strategically, the activist foreign policy of the United States increased after the September 11 terror attacks, causing widespread suspicion in China that the United States is bent on containing China. China's threats toward

---

[1] "U.S., China Stand Against Terrorism, Remarks by President Bush and President Jiang Zemin," White House press release, October 19, 2001.

[2] "President Bush Meets with Chinese President Jiang Zemin," White House press release, February 21, 2002.

Taiwan and its close relations with rogue states, on the other hand, have led many in the United States to believe that China's authoritarian regime is bent on undermining U.S. interests where it can. We next illustrate these concerns and assess their impact on U.S.-China military relations.

Global War on Terrorism (GWOT)

China's public support for the GWOT has been timely and consistently strong. Beijing immediately condemned the September 11 attacks on the United States,[3] and Chinese President Jiang Zemin was quick to call President Bush to express his condolences.[4] Diplomatically, China supported U.S. strikes in Afghanistan with a caution that they be against "clearly defined targets" and "avoid innocent casualties."[5] China also voted in favor of the UN Security Council resolution against terrorism, which was "the first time that China has voted in favor of authorizing the international use of force."[6] The United States and China have held numerous sessions of counterterrorism dialogue that are described by the U.S. State Department as having produced results that were "encouraging and concrete."[7] In addition to sharing intelligence, China has also "approved establishment of an FBI legal attaché in Beijing and agreed to create a U.S.-China counterterrorism working group on financing and law enforcement."[8] During Operation Enduring Freedom, China increased the number of troops on its border with Afghanistan and Pakistan to prevent terrorists from entering China and conducted a search of Chinese banks

---

[3] See "FM Spokesman: Chinese Government Condemns Terrorism," *People's Daily* (online), September 12, 2001.

[4] "Chinese, U.S. Presidents Talk Over Phone," *People's Daily* (online), September 13, 2001.

[5] Zlex Frew McMillan and Major Garrett, "U.S. Wins Support From China," *CNN.com*, October 19, 2001.

[6] U.S. Department of State, *Global Patterns of Terrorism 2001*, May 21, 2002.

[7] Ibid.

[8] Ibid.

to determine if terrorists had used them for funding.[9] China and the United States have also signed a declaration of principles to allow U.S. Customs agents to inspect containers at the ports of Shanghai and Shenzhen.[10]

Perhaps the most important assistance that China has provided the United States is its support of Pakistan, a long-time friend of China.[11] Immediately after September 11, the PRC dispatched Vice Foreign Minister Wang Yi, helping to shore up Pakistan's decision to join the global coalition against terrorism and the Taliban.[12] After a five-day trip to Beijing in December 2001, Pakistani President Pervez Musharraf stated that "Chinese leaders showed complete under-standing and support to the rationale behind Pakistan joining the in-ternational coalition to fight terrorism in Afghanistan and around the world."[13] China has also been helpful in easing tensions between In-dia and Pakistan so that the conflict in Kashmir does not disrupt op-erations in Afghanistan. U.S. Secretary of State Colin Powell has stated that "China has not tried to be a spoiler but instead tried to help the United States alleviate tensions and convince the two parties to scale down their dangerous confrontation."[14]

U.S.-China cooperation in support of the GWOT has had lim-its, however. Beijing has expressed concern that the United States does not completely support its efforts to stop terrorism in the Mus-lim region of Xinjiang, warning that there should be "no double standards" in the war on terror. Foreign Ministry spokesman Sun

---

[9] Ibid.

[10] Russel Barling, "China Joins U.S. Drive to Secure Container Trade; Shanghai and Shenzhen Are the First Mainland Ports to Sign the Initiative," *South China Morning Post*, July 30, 2003.

[11] David M. Lampton and Richard Daniel Ewing, *U.S.-China Relations in a Post–September 11th World*, Washington, D.C.: The Nixon Center, 2002, p. 62.

[12] "China's Minister to Pakistan," Pakistan Newswire, September 18, 2001.

[13] "Musharaff Says Complete Unanimity of Sino-Pak Views on Key Issues," Pakistan Newswire, December 25, 2001.

[14] "Powell Praises China's Role in Reducing Indo-Pakistan Tensions," *Press Trust of India*, April 25, 2002.

Yuxi stated that China "hopes that efforts to fight against East Turke-
stan terrorist forces will become part of the international efforts and
should also win support and understanding."[15] The United States, for
its part, "accepts the fact that there are people from western China
that are involved in terrorist activities in Afghanistan, and that terrorists' actions have hurt . . . but it does not believe that all of the
people of western China are indeed terrorists."[16] These concerns,
however, may have been allayed by the designation of the East Turke-
stan Islamic Movement (ETIM) as a terrorist organization by the
United States according to Executive Order 13224, although ETIM
was not placed on the State Department foreign terrorist organization
list.[17]

At the same time, China has not supported an expansion of the
war on terror against states described as the "axis of evil" (Iraq, Iran,
and North Korea) and specifically stated its opposition to the invasion of Iraq. On November 8, 2002, China voted for UN Resolution
1441, which gave Iraq "a final opportunity to comply with its disar-
mament obligations"[18] and stated "that the Council has repeatedly
warned Iraq that it will face serious consequences as a result of its

---

[15] "No Double Standards in Anti-Terror Fight, Says China of Domestic Unrest," *AFP*, October 11, 2001.

[16] "U.S. Envoy Hails 'Resolute' China But Denies Xinjiang Terror Claims," *Deutsche Press-
Agentur*, December 6, 2001.

[17] Executive Order 13224 was issued by the White House on September 23, 2001. To
qualify as a terrorist organization a group must have committed, or pose a significant risk of
committing, acts of terrorism that threaten the security of U.S. nationals or the national
security, foreign policy, or economy of the United States; be owned or controlled by, or to
act for or on behalf of those persons; be determined to be a terrorist organization by the Secretary of the Treasury, in consultation with the Secretary of State and the Attorney General
and with consultations with foreign authorities; assist in, sponsor, or provide financial, material, or technological support for, or financial or other services to or in support of, such acts
of terrorism or be otherwise associated with people listed in the Order's Annex. The U.S.
State Department's list of Foreign Terrorist Organizations is more restrictive in that it requires approval by Congress.

[18] "United Nations Security Council Resolution 1441," November 8, 2002, p. 3.

continued violations of its obligations."[19] Since that time, however, it consistently voiced its opposition to the war.[20]

China is also apprehensive about the geopolitical ramifications of the GWOT. Most important, it is concerned that the newly enhanced relationships between the United States and the Central Asian states, Pakistan, and India could be used to surround and contain China. In addition, China is concerned that the GWOT could be used by Japan as justification to expand its military participation in international coalitions.[21] At least one Chinese security analyst has speculated that "perhaps after the war on terrorism, this newly mobilized order will re-aim at China."[22] Some in China have also expressed disquiet with what they perceive as Washington's unilateralism in the war on terrorism. In response to the "axis of evil," one Chinese scholar has written that

> before the Afghan war could end completely, the United States has determined new targets for its war against terror. However, the United States has not solicited the opinions of any countries in the coalition against terror. The United States has still persisted in its old way even when the EU nations and other allies criticized it. . . . It is totally up to the United States to say who are the foes and who are the friends.[23]

Another Chinese author has concluded that the United States is using the war on terror to bring "the whole world into the political order

---

[19] "United Nations Security Council . . .," p. 5.

[20] See, for example, "China's Stance and Diplomatic Effort to Solve Iraq Issue," *People's Daily* (online), March 3, 2003.

[21] "China Urges Japan to Be Prudent in Aiding Fight Against Terrorism," *People's Daily* (online), September 28, 2001.

[22] Andrew Higgins and Charles Hutzler, "Chinese Goals Take a Backseat As U.S. Rises to the Fore in Asia," *Wall Street Journal*, October 19, 2001.

[23] Liu Jianfei, "Listen for 'Fizz'—Empires Decline Not with Bang But with Fizz; Unilateralism Is Equally Dangerous to United States," *Shijie Zhishi*, May 1, 2002, pp. 16–17 in FBIS as "PRC Journal on US Unilateralism, Decline of Great Powers," May 16, 2002.

led by the United States. This alone is where the real meaning of the American war on terrorism lies."[24]

Taiwan

China's discomfort with many of the aspects of the U.S. war on terrorism, however, is only one of many issues that makes Beijing extremely suspicious of U.S. strategy around the globe. First and foremost is U.S. policy toward Taiwan. China views Taiwan as a part of the territory of the People's Republic of China that would have been recovered in the 1950s had the United States not intervened. China has not renounced the use of force in its attempts to convince Taiwan to unify. It also believes that Taiwan's continuing refusal to unify with the mainland is a direct result of U.S. military support in the form of arms sales. China believes that one reason for the U.S. support of Taiwan is to prevent China from becoming a regional power. The United States, on its part, has stated that it desires a peaceful resolution of the issue, has expressed opposition to the use of force by China to resolve the problem, and has stated that the United States does not support Taiwan independence, but does not necessarily oppose it either.[25]

Beijing is particularly concerned with the increasingly "official" nature of U.S. policy toward Taiwan. In April 2001, President Bush stated that the United States would "do whatever it takes" to defend Taiwan from a Chinese attack, although he added a qualifier that the United States did not support Taiwan independence.[26] In March 2002, Taiwan Defense Minister Tang Yiao-ming attended a conference held in the United States entitled "The United States-Taiwan

---

[24] Pu Qibi, "The U.S. Has Profited from 9.11," *Shijie Zhishi*, May 1, 2002, pp. 22–23 in FBIS as "PRC Journal Article Claims US Gains 'Strategic Benefits' From War on Terrorism," May 16, 2002.

[25] "Taiwan Says Armitage's Clarification on U.S. Policy Conducive to Regional Peace," *BBC*, August 27, 2002.

[26] "Bush Vows 'To Do Whatever It Takes' To Defend Taiwan," *CNN.com*, April 25, 2001.

Defense Summit, 2002." This was the first time that a Taiwanese defense minister had traveled to the United States other than for transit
since 1979. During this conference U.S. Deputy Secretary of Defense
Paul Wolfowitz repeated President Bush's pledge that the United
States would do whatever it takes to defend Taiwan.[27] In response,
the Chinese summoned the U.S. ambassador to protest the atten-
dance of Tang at the conference.[28] China has also protested the increased amount of arms that has been approved for sale to Taiwan,
especially diesel submarines.[29]

The Use of Force, Unilateralism, and "Hegemony"

China is also opposed to the use of force when it is not supported by
the United Nations. It was opposed to the use of force in Kosovo on
the grounds that it infringed on state sovereignty and was executed
without UN Security Council approval. China remains critical of
U.S. intentions in this area because of the Clinton policy to use force
to protect human rights and because this use of force set a precedent
that could be used against China to improve its human rights, especially in Xinjiang and Tibet. Beijing has asserted that the real goal of
this "new interventionism" is "aimed at promoting hegemonism and
building a new order of international relations that benefits the West"
and that by "preaching new interventionism, the West is simply
challenging and negating the sovereignty and the rights of existence
and development of the developing countries; under the pretext of
'universal human values.'"[30]

---

[27] Andrea Shalal-Esa, "U.S. Vows to Do What It Takes to Aid Taiwan Defense," *Reuters,*
April 9, 2002.

[28] "China Summons U.S. Ambassador to Make Representations," *People's Daily* (online),
March 18, 2002.

[29] "China Strongly Protests U.S. Arms Sales to Taiwan," *People's Daily* (online), April 25,
2001.

[30] Yuan Zhibing, "What Is 'New' About New Interventionism," *People's Daily*, July 29,
1999, p. 6.

In addition, China is concerned about U.S. unilateralism and what it sees as U.S. hegemonism more generally. China opposed the U.S. withdrawal from the Antiballistic Missile (ABM) Treaty and continues to criticize U.S. missile defense plans. It has called the ABM Treaty the cornerstone of nuclear arms control and has expressed the belief that the U.S. withdrawal from the treaty will force China to increase its nuclear weapons arsenal. It regards missile defenses as a U.S. effort for "absolute" protection that can then be used to blackmail China. China is also concerned with press reporting of the newly revised Nuclear Posture Review (NPR), which described the United States as preparing for nuclear strikes against six countries, including China. China sees the NPR as a threat; in their view, it indicates that the United States may threaten the use of nuclear weapons to prevent China from using force against Taiwan.[31]

China's Response

China's concerns with the U.S. willingness to use force, U.S. support for Taiwan, and U.S. development of an alliance system that could be used against China have led many in the PRC to believe that the United States has already identified Beijing as an enemy and that Washington's mixture of engagement and containment is increasingly focused on containing instead of engaging China. What has been described as "an eastward shift"[32] of U.S. strategy is exemplified by the *Quadrennial Defense Review* (QDR) released in September 2001. According to the QDR, "the possibility exists that a military competitor with a formidable resource base will emerge in the region."[33] In re-

---

[31] Zhou Rong, "Can a New Nuclear Strategy Guarantee US Security?" *Shijie Zhishi*, May 1, 2002, pp. 20–21 in FBIS as "PRC Journal Questions Whether Changes in US Nuclear Strategy Can Guarantee Security," May 16, 2002.

[32] Niu Jun, "Shocks Bring About Change," *Xiandai Guoji Guanxi*, March 20, 2002, pp. 16–17 in FBIS as "PRC Scholar Discusses Impact of 11 September on US Position in World US Strategy," May 2, 2002.

[33] U.S. Department of Defense, *Quadrennial Defense Review*, September 30, 2001, p. 4.

sponse, the Defense Department has decided that it "will increase aircraft carrier battlegroup presence in the Western Pacific and will explore options for homeporting an additional three to four surface combatants, and guided cruise missile submarines (SSGNs), in that area."[34] This led one Chinese scholar to write, "There is no need for us to shy away from saying that this strategic readjustment naturally includes a focus on China, and that this is a fairly significant part of their intentions."[35]

The combination of these factors has led some Chinese scholars and officials to conclude that the U.S. war on terrorism does not present an opportunity for fundamentally better cooperation between the United States and China. Rather, China must still face this relationship with a certain amount of ambivalence. As another Chinese scholar states:

> Because the [11 September] incident showed that at least China was not a direct threat to the United States, the U.S. domestic political debate on China policy could be controlled or concealed to some extent. However, the fundamental and potential state of strategic tension between China and the United States has not changed. The damaging nature of the Taiwan issue has not changed. Because U.S. unilateralism has further reared its head, there is still great uncertainty in relations between the two countries.[36]

In response to a U.S. strategy that it sees as infringing on its sovereignty and national interests, China has developed its own world vision that seeks to limit hegemony and unilateralism, called the "New Security Concept." This model, developed in 1997, states that relations between countries should be established on the basis of the Five Principles of Peaceful Coexistence: mutual respect for territorial

---

[34] *Quadrennial Defense Review*, p. 27.

[35] Niu Jun, "Shocks Bring About Change."

[36] Jin Canrong, "Great Power Relations from a Comparative Perspective," *Xiandai Guoji Guanxi*, March 20, 2002, pp. 14–16 in FBIS as "PRC Scholar Analyzes US, Great Power Relations," May 2, 2002.

integrity and sovereignty, mutual non-aggression, non-interference in each other's internal affairs, equality and mutual benefit, and peaceful coexistence. According to China,

> these are the political basis and premise of global and regional security. Each country has the right to choose its own social system, development strategy, and way of life and no other country should interfere in the internal affairs of any other country in any way or under any pretext, much less resort to military threats or aggression.[37]

The New Security Concept also states that

> all countries should promote mutual understanding and trust through dialogue and cooperation and seek the settlement of divergences and disputes among nations through peaceful means. These are the realistic ways to guarantee peace and security. Security is mutual and security dialogues and cooperation should be aimed at promoting trust, not at creating confrontations, still less at directing the spearhead against a third country or infringing upon the security interests of any other nation.[38]

These principles seem innocuous enough, but as David Finkelstein points out, the New Security Concept is an "indication of China's dissatisfaction, or even frustration, with the current international system."[39] China has frequently expressed the hope that, after the Cold War, the world would no longer be ruled by the bipolar relations of the United States and the Soviet Union, but that instead multiple sources of power and influence would replace the current unipolar world. This belief "appears to be a direct Chinese reaction to policies and actions by the United States in the last few years that un-

---

[37] Information Office of the State Council of the People's Republic of China, *China's National Defense*, July 1998.

[38] Ibid.

[39] David M. Finkelstein, *China's New Security Concept: Reading Between the Lines*, Alexandria, VA: Center for Naval Analyses Corporation, April 1999, p. 5.

nerve, unsettle and are perceived as threatening by Beijing."[40] In this sense, the New Security Concept can be viewed as a counter to the need for a forward presence of U.S. military forces, U.S. military alliances, and what China sees as U.S. interventionism, which can manifest itself as anything from verbal criticism to military attack. It may also be viewed as a reaction to the expansion of NATO, NATO's intervention in the Balkans, and the proposed expansion of the Partnership for Peace. Third, it is a reaction to the continuing superiority of U.S. military power and its continued role as the sole superpower. Finally, the New Security Concept is a reaction to the Clinton-Hashimoto Joint Statement in April 1996 and the promulgation in 1997 of the U.S.-Japan Revised Guidelines for Defense Cooperation.[41] Finkelstein has concluded that "one might ask if the New Security Concept bespeaks China's 'New Insecurity.' If so, this new insecurity is a combination of two factors—China's increasing interdependence in the world and a world order dominated by the United States as sole superpower."[42]

Because the global visions of the two countries appear to be nearly diametrically opposed, it should come as no surprise that their defense policies are also strikingly different. According to China's 2002 defense white paper, China's defense policy is "defensive in nature" and is concerned with "safeguarding state sovereignty, unity, territorial integrity and security; upholding economic development. . . ." China also states that it will not join any military bloc or crave for any sphere of influence. China also states that it is strategically defense-oriented and will strike only after the enemy has struck.[43]

On the other hand, U.S. defense policy is much more proactive. According to the *Quadrennial Defense Review*, one goal of U.S. de-

---

[40] Finkelstein, p. 6.

[41] Finkelstein, pp. 6–7.

[42] Finkelstein, p. 7.

[43] Information Office of the State Council of the People's Republic of China, *China's National Defense in 2002*, December 9, 2002.

fense policy is to assure allies and friends by promoting security cooperation that will "create favorable balances of military power in critical areas of the world to deter aggression or coercion."[44] This cooperation includes "enhancing interoperability and peacetime
preparations for coalition operations, as well as increasing allied participation in activities such as joint and combined training and experimentation."[45] To deter threats and coercion against U.S. interests,
an emphasis will be placed on "peacetime forward deterrence in critical areas of the world that will require enhancing the future capability
of forward deployed and stationed forces, coupled with global intelligence, strike, and information assets."[46] In addition, in *The National
Security Strategy of the United States of America,* released in 2002, the
U.S. government stated that the United States will act preemp-
tively.[47]

China's strategy, therefore, is primarily focused on threats to its
territorial security and is less focused on defending its national interest in areas away from its borders, while the United States seeks to
defend its national interests globally. In fact, the U.S. Defense Department states that the QDR "restores the defense of the United
States as the Department's primary mission,"[48] implying that in previous years the defense of the United States was secondary to international concerns. This basic fundamental dichotomy between the two
defense policies can be explained by the differing positions of the two
countries in the world hierarchy. China is a developing, authoritarian
nation that is considered a rising regional power. Its primary concern
is economic development. Consequently, for China to rapidly develop a military with global reach would not only stretch the capabilities of the PLA, but would also divert resources that are needed for

---

[44] *Quadrennial Defense Review*, p. 11.

[45] *Quadrennial Defense Review*, p. 15.

[46] *Quadrennial Defense Review*, p. 12.

[47] White House, *The National Security Strategy of the United States of America*, September 2002.

[48] *Quadrennial Defense Review*, p. 17.

economic development. Others may also argue that China's foreign policy is inherently non-expansionist and will remain so regardless of its economic power.[49] The United States, on the other hand, is a democratic, lone superpower with global interests and the ability to act in those interests.

This dichotomy has led both sides to search for a common purpose in an attempt to minimize confrontation. While agreements exist on the principles of trade issues and some areas of regional security (e.g., a nonnuclear Korean peninsula), significant unresolved issues remain over human rights, proliferation, and Taiwan. One scholar has described the United States and China as strategic competitors because "both Washington and Beijing hedge against each other. . . . Beijing builds its ties with Moscow, while Washington strengthens its alliances and security partnerships around China."[50] While the world visions of the two countries may be at odds, it may be useful to further define the relationship by making a distinction between "strategic competitors" and "strategic adversaries." Strategic competitors "can cooperate in certain, limited areas . . . while having competitive and sometimes contentious relations in the main."[51] "Strategic adversaries," on the other hand, would more accurately describe the relationship between the United States and the Soviet Union when those two countries engaged in efforts to achieve global dominance.[52] Thus, strategic competition does not necessarily preclude the two countries from engaging in cooperative activities, including military-to-military relations. Although limited cooperation may be possible in regard to the war on terrorism, this type of relationship would suggest that the bulk of activities should be conducted to reduce the likelihood of

---

[49] For a discussion of the development of China's national strategy, see Michael D. Swaine and Ashley J. Tellis, *Interpreting China's Grand Strategy: Past, Present and Future*, MR-1121-AF, Santa Monica: RAND Corporation, 2000.

[50] David Shambaugh, "Sino-American Strategic Relations: From Partners to Competitors," *Survival*, Spring 2000, p. 99.

[51] Shambaugh, p. 99.

[52] Shambaugh, p. 99.

conflict, such as dialogue, and to increase the U.S. military's knowledge of the PLA in the event of armed conflict.

CHAPTER FOUR

The U.S. Debate over U.S.-China Military Relations[1]

The current U.S. debate surrounding U.S.-China military relations has centered around four major issues: the potential risks of U.S.-China military relations to U.S. national security; the potential benefits of the U.S.-China military relationship to the United States; the ability of the United States to influence China; and the relative levels of reciprocity and transparency in the relationship. The issues of reciprocity and transparency in particular are central to the Defense Department's current restrictions. The Clinton administration, in contrast, emphasized the ability of military relations to influence China. This chapter examines each of these arguments and assesses their validity.

Have U.S.-China Military Relations Harmed U.S. National Security?

During the 1980s, a significant aspect of U.S. military relations with China was to assist the PLA in its modernization efforts. As we discussed earlier, the United States assisted the PLA under the umbrella of providing a strategic counterweight to the Soviet Union. For ex-

---

[1] Much of the information in this chapter is derived from interviews with people who have studied or who have been intimately involved in the U.S.-China military-to-military relationship. All prefer to remain anonymous.

ample, after the normalization of relations in 1979, U.S. military leaders provided copies of Field Manual 100-5, *Air-Land Battle*, to their PLA counterparts. The PLA then used the manual in their own experimentation with combined arms operations.[2]

During the 1990s, however, China was no longer needed as a strategic counterweight to the defunct Soviet Union. Instead, U.S. attention turned to the PLA's role in repressing China's population and its ability to threaten its neighbors. During the 1990s, it was not the expressed policy of the United States to assist the PLA's modernization. Rather, cooperation with the PLA was seen as providing a window for China to observe international practices that would then encourage it to conform to international standards. As the relationship expanded in the 1990s, however, more attention was focused on the potential harm to U.S. national security that might result from the military relationship with China. Some interlocutors assert that the PLA has benefited from contacts with the U.S. military and that these contacts have improved the ability of the PLA to conduct warfighting. Consequently, an improved PLA would be better able to attack Taiwanese and U.S. forces in the event of a military conflict over Taiwan. Other interlocutors argue that the threat has been exaggerated. They point out that briefings given to the PLA are unclassified and general in nature and are of little value in improving its combat abilities. Still others argue that for the U.S. military to access information about the PLA, it must be open to some degree so that the PLA also benefits from mutual exchanges.

Determining whether the PLA has benefited from contacts with the U.S. military is based largely on inference, but there are indications that the PLA has improved its warfighting capability as a result. For example, logistics is of particular concern to the PLA. During the Korean War, the inability of the PLA to keep its troops well supplied seriously affected its operations. Currently, the PLA describes high-technology warfare as consuming large quantities of ammunition and

---

[2] Kenneth W. Allen and Eric A. McVadon, *China's Foreign Military Relations*, Henry L. Stimson Center, October 1999, p. 39.

supplies. Logistics reform, then, is key to the PLA's ability to fight a modern war.

The PLA's approach to logistics reform is noted to be similar to the U.S. military's. PLA delegations have received briefings on U.S. military logistics and have toured the FedEx operations center in Memphis, Tennessee. Most of the PLA's knowledge of the U.S. logistics systems, however, is "probably due to the PLA's study of DoD logistics material readily available through the government printing office and open-source publications."[3] However, discussions with U.S. officials have provided a better understanding of the U.S. approach to logistics. Consequently, the PLA has "definitely learned a considerable amount from their interaction with U.S. and other foreign military logistics officials."[4]

An examination of questions the PLA asked while on trips to the United States also reveals the possibility that the Chinese military may have benefited from discussions with their U.S. counterparts—depending, of course, on the answers it received. In one visit by the General Logistics Department of the PLA, Chinese participants asked the following questions: "How are the U.S. logistics departments organized? How do they function in wartime? How are they modernizing? What are the most prominent logistics problems facing the Army?"[5] Depending on how the questions were answered, it is possible that these types of discussions not only assisted PLA modernization, but also helped it to identify weak points in the U.S. logistics system that could be exploited during combat.

Again, these examples provide no definitive proof that the PLA benefited from exchanges. The U.S. military publishes a large amount of open source material, and it is possible that much of the knowledge about the U.S. military could come from a systematic review of this information. Most joint doctrine publications, for instance, were

---

[3] Allen and McVadon, p. 36.

[4] Allen and McVadon, p. 36.

[5] U.S. Department of Defense, *Report of Past Military to Military Exchanges and Contacts Between the U.S. and PRC.*

available on the Internet prior to September 11, 2001. In addition, the PLA could have gained information from other countries' militaries, such as the United Kingdom and Turkey. It is possible, however, that allowing PLA officers to question U.S. military personnel about things they have read has increased the PLA's understanding of the U.S. military, benefiting the PLA's modernization efforts as well as increasing its awareness of U.S. operational planning. The PLA could then better develop strategies to counter U.S. military moves. In addition, the PLA is one of the more insular organizations of the Chinese Communist Party. Its members are often very conservative and have little knowledge of the outside world. As a result, exposure to modern militaries can provide benchmarks for the PLA and information on the limits of the possible. President Jiang Zemin echoed these thoughts when in February 2002 he encouraged PLA officers to learn more about foreign militaries, saying "military students who study abroad enable the CMC [Central Military Commission] to know the development of foreign militaries and the modernization requirements of our army. . . ."[6]

An additional measure of whether the PLA benefits from interactions with the U.S. military is its own opinion of the value of the relationship. According to one analysis, the PLA considers functional exchanges to be a very important, although not the most important, aspect of its interactions with the U.S. military. The PLA views functional exchanges as important because it "is under pressure from its own leadership to move forward with its reform programs and the United States has tremendous potential value-added to those responsible for formulating new ways of doing business."[7] Thus, the fact the PLA values functional exchanges for their usefulness in pushing re-

---

[6] *Xinhua*, "Jiang Zemin huijian quanjun junshi liuxue gongzuo huiyi daibiao" (Jiang Zemin Meets with Representatives from the All-Army Study Abroad Working Meeting), February 23, 2002.

[7] David M. Finkelstein and John Unangst, *Engaging DoD: Chinese Perspectives on Military Relations with the United States*, Alexandria, VA: Center for Naval Analyses Corporation, October 1999, p. 32.

form suggests that it has benefited from functional exchanges with the U.S. military.

Have Military Relations with China Benefited the United States?

The flip side of the debate is whether the U.S. military has benefited from these exchanges. Any benefit is made difficult by the PLA's penchant for secrecy and deception. NDU and National War College visits to China do give future general and flag-grade officers exposure to China that they otherwise might not have had. Officers with minimal knowledge of China have benefited from these activities, even those at show-case units. For example, a trip report from a Naval War College visit revealed that the participants learned that there were various schools of thought in China about the Revolution in Military Affairs (RMA).[8] Finally, interlocutors have provided examples of information gathered on the PLA through delegation visits or through the normal function of the attaché office, although the value of these reports cannot be assessed in an unclassified study.

U.S. Influence on the PLA

An oft-cited argument for engaging the PLA is to develop contacts and lines of communication so that the United States can articulate its policies and concerns, influence the Chinese policymaking process, and develop relationships with PLA officers. In times of crisis the United States will then have a point of contact even when other lines of communication may have been shut off.[9] Proponents of engagement also insist that, in order for China to develop into a responsible member of the international community, a dialogue must be maintained to find areas of agreement and to reduce tensions in areas of

---

[8] U.S. Department of Defense, *Report of Past Military to Military Exchanges and Contacts Between the U.S. and PRC.*

[9] See, for example, Ashton Carter and William J. Perry, *Preventive Defense: A New Security Strategy for America*, Washington, D.C.: Brookings Institution Press, 1999, pp. 106–111.

disagreement. In this way it will be possible to encourage positive developments in China. Those who believe the United States can influence China stress that China's increasing economic, political, and military power may make it more active in international affairs. China is a UN Security Council member that can frustrate or at least strongly influence U.S. actions in that forum. They also point out that China, as the self-proclaimed leader of the developing world, may have the ability to influence the policies of other developing countries. In particular, the United States needs China's assistance in dealing with North Korea. Moreover, China's continuing proliferation activities make it necessary to sensitize China to U.S. concerns.[10] Finally, high-level engagement with China can communicate U.S. resolve in case of a conflict over Taiwan.

Implicit in these arguments is the assumption that the United States can influence China through its military relationship with the PLA. With prolonged interaction, proponents believe engagement can persuade the Chinese to be more open about its strategic intentions and procurement, budgeting, and operating procedures as well as lessen misunderstanding.[11] Functional military contacts can also play a deterrent role by showing the PLA not only U.S. technological prowess but also the professionalism and competency of U.S. military personnel.

Others believe the United States has only limited influence with China. They believe, like the first group, that high-level dialogue with China is useful for conveying strategic intentions, resolving misunderstandings, and reinforcing deterrence. In addition, professional military exchanges are a good way to expose each country's military officers to one another. They may also agree that Track 2 exchanges[12] between academics and nongovernment personnel may be useful in informing both sides of each country's thoughts and intentions and

---

[10] Thomas L. Wilborn, p. 8.

[11] These points are taken from William H. Perry, 1995.

[12] Track 1 meetings involve only government representatives. Track 1.5 meetings involve government and nongovernmental representatives. Track 2 meetings involve nongovernmental representatives only.

that meetings such as the MMCA can be useful in developing a code of conduct between the two militaries. However, this group will caution that seeking personal relationships with PLA officers or otherwise attempting to develop relationships so the United States will have a point of contact during crises will probably fail. They also believe that China, like all countries, will act only in its own interests and often these interests are counter to U.S. interests. Thus, China cannot be expected to take U.S. concerns into account.

A third group believes the United States has no ability to influence China and, like the second group, believes that China will act according to its own domestic political dynamic and in accord with its own national security interests. It believes military ties have been ineffective in reducing tensions or in building confidence. While some people may not disagree with holding high-level talks with the PLA, they do not believe the United States will benefit from these exchanges. They also believe the United States does not need to show the PLA its muscle in order to deter China. Rather, U.S. performance in Operations Desert Storm, Allied Force, Enduring Freedom, and Iraqi Freedom has done more to show U.S. military capability than have PLA visits to U.S. military bases.

The debate on the U.S. influence on the PLA and China, therefore, mainly centers around two questions: has the United States influenced China in the past and is it possible to influence China in the future? History, unfortunately, reveals the United States has limited ability to influence the PLA. In particular, the U.S.-China relationship has witnessed some notable failures that call into question whether the U.S. military can effectively communicate with their Chinese counterparts in crisis situations. In December 1994, a U.S. military helicopter was shot down over North Korea, resulting in the death of one of the pilots. Secretary of Defense William Perry was unable to secure Chinese cooperation to work for the release of the pilots until the Chinese were tricked into having a meeting they thought was on another topic. In March 1996 during the Taiwan missile crisis, Perry and Secretary of State Warren Christopher met with Chinese Vice Minister of Foreign Affairs Liu Huaqiu to persuade China not to fire a second round of missiles near the coast of

Taiwan. During this meeting Perry told Liu that "the United States has more than enough military capability to protect its vital national security interests in the region, and is prepared to demonstrate that" and that he "believed that a repeat of the missile firings would be a political blunder and in time would come to be seen as such even in China."[13] Perry's meeting with Liu did not persuade China to stop its missile operations and China conducted one more missile firing.

A final example of the failure of U.S. influence is the inability of Ambassador Joseph Prueher to find contacts within the PLA during the EP-3 crisis. According to many interlocutors, Ambassador Prueher had extensively cultivated contacts within the PLA during his tour as the combatant commander of U.S. Pacific Command. However, during the EP-3 crisis, Prueher was unable to reach these PLA contacts; in the words of one person, "no one would answer his calls," although he was able to establish contact with his usual diplomatic interlocutor Assistant Foreign Minister Zhou Wenzhong late on the day of the incident.[14] These examples suggest that during times of crisis the United States has failed to leverage previous contacts to influence China, has been unable to discuss issues with the Chinese except through trickery, or has been unable to establish communication with individuals with whom the United States has had a relationship.

If the United States has been unsuccessful in influencing China during crisis situations, have there been any successes? In a multilateral context, China has reacted positively to suggestions by states within the region to become more transparent about its military affairs. In November 1995 China published its first white paper on arms control, and in July 1998 it published its first white paper on defense, followed by others in October 2000 and December 2002. These white papers are less revealing than those of Japan or Taiwan, but are nevertheless good initial efforts to increase transparency.[15]

---

[13] Carter and Perry, p. 96.

[14] John Keefe, "A Tale of 'Two Very Sorries' Redux," *Far Eastern Economic Review* (online), March 21, 2002.

[15] Bates Gill and Evan S. Medeiros, "The Foreign and Domestic Influences on China's Arms Control and Nonproliferation Policies," *China Quarterly*, March 2000, p. 80; Evan S.

In regard to the effective use of unilateral U.S. influence, the U.S. military is said to have played a role in negotiating China's assistance in resolving the North Korean nuclear crisis in 1994.[16] The United States has also been effective in demonstrating its military power. The PLA does respect the U.S. military, not only because of its advanced weaponry but also because of the professionalism of its personnel. PLA officers are impressed, for example, that U.S. noncommissioned officers often perform duties assigned to officers in the PLA. To what extent functional exchanges have formed this impression is unknown; certainly the effective prosecution of combat operations since 1991 by the U.S. military has had an effect on Chinese perceptions. Chinese military writings refer to the Gulf War as the "epitome" of modern war. At the very least then, functional exchanges have undoubtedly had a reinforcing effect. Still, U.S. efforts to deter China may be only partially successful. They have not dissuaded China from developing or acquiring weapon systems that appear to be for potential use against the U.S. military. In addition, while the Chinese do not doubt U.S. military power, they do doubt American political resolve to use and sustain the use of this power in the face of casualties. Thus, merely displaying U.S. military power does not address whether the United States has the political will to use it.

A look back at these past successes and failures in U.S.-China military interactions may help determine the future efficacy of U.S. efforts to influence the PLA. Further, is the dynamic described above limited to the U.S.-China military relationship or has the United States been able to exercise its influence in other areas that may give us insight into how to better manage the military relationship? To better understand U.S. influence on China, it is therefore useful to look at two other areas where the United States and China have had a

Medeiros, "Through a Red Glass Darkly," *Far Eastern Economic Review*, November 9, 2000, p. 36.

[16] Jer Donald Get, "What's with the Relationship Between America's Army and China's PLA?" *Strategic Studies Institute*, September 15, 1996, pp. 14–15.

contentious relationship: intellectual property rights (IPR) and nonproliferation and arms control.

Intellectual Property Rights. Piracy in China continues to be rampant. In 2001, for example, it is estimated that U.S. industry lost more than $1.5 billion in pirated movies, CDs, software, and books,[17] despite four bilateral agreements between China and the United States since 1991. The United States in 1991, 1995, and 1996 threatened trade sanctions against China if it did not improve IPR laws and enforcement. Since 1996, disputes over IPR violations have narrowed and diminished, perhaps partly because of better incentives for the Chinese government to protect its own industries. Chinese businesses and individuals have an increased stake in protecting their own rights. In addition, China had to demonstrate its commitment to improving protection of intellectual property prior to its entry into the World Trade Organization (WTO), without which the United States would not have approved China's accession. However, according to scholars, "the reduced conflict over IPRs after 1995 has not occurred because piracy has been curtailed in China—it remains a significant problem. Instead it reflects the recognition by the U.S. government that the Chinese government had changed the priority assigned to strengthening its IPR institutions to meet [WTO] standards."[18]

Arms Control and Nonproliferation. Arms control and nonproliferation is another longstanding issue of contention between the United States and China. In the past, China has exported nuclear technology, chemical and missile goods, and technology to Iran, Pakistan, and other countries. The record shows that over time China's view of the importance of arms control and proliferation has been evolving toward an acceptance of international standards. For

---

[17] International Intellectual Property Alliance web page release, http://www.iipa.com/rbc/2002/2002SPEC301PRC.pdf.

[18] The information about the U.S.-China dispute over IPR is taken from Sumner J. La Croix and Denise Eby Konan, "Intellectual Property Rights in China: The Changing Political Economy of Chinese-American Interests," *The World Economy*, June 2002, pp. 759–788. The quote is taken from page 785.

example, in 1968 China refused to enter into the Nuclear Nonproliferation Treaty (NPT) on the grounds that it was a "conspiracy con-
cocted by the USSR and the U.S. to maintain their nuclear monop-
oly."[19] Since then China has joined the NPT as well as the Chemical
Weapons Convention (CWC) and the Biological Weapons Convention (BWC) and has signed the Comprehensive Test Ban Treaty
(CTBT). While changes in China's national security interests and its
perceptions of international security affairs have influenced the shifts
in Beijing's proliferation policies, U.S. policy has also played a role.[20]
In 1991, in response to U.S. economic sanctions for missile sales to
Pakistan, China agreed to abide by the original Guidelines and Parameters of the Missile Technology Control Regime (MTCR), although it still has not become a member.[21] The United States may
have also been successful in sensitizing China to U.S. concerns about
Iran's nuclear program. In addition, in September 1997, a month
before a summit between Presidents Clinton and Jiang, China
pledged not to export C-801 and C-802 antiship missiles to Iran or
to provide new nuclear assistance to Iran.[22] More recently, in August
2002, two months before a summit between Presidents Bush and Jiang, China published an export control list to better manage transfers
of missile components.[23] Despite China's official commitments, its
adherence to many of its arms control and nonproliferation pledges is
still in doubt. A 2001 Defense Department report, for example,

---

[19] "Nuclear Nonproliferation Treaty," *China Profiles Database*, http://www.nti.org/db/
china/nptorg.htm.

[20] See Evan S. Medeiros, "Integrating a Rising Power into Global Nonproliferation Regimes:
U.S.-China Negotiations and Interactions on Nonproliferation, 1980–2001," unpublished
Ph.D. dissertation, London: London School of Economics, July 2002.

[21] Wendy Frieman, "New Members of the Club: Chinese Participation In Arms Control
Regimes 1980–1995," *Nonproliferation Review*, Spring/Summer 1996, p. 20.

[22] Center for Nonproliferation Studies, *China Profiles Database*, "China's Missile Assistance
and Exports to Iran," and "China's Nuclear Exports and Assistance to Iran,"
http://www.nti.org/db/china/miranpos.htm and http://www.nti.org/db/china/miranpos.
htm.

[23] Phillip P. Pan, "China Issues Rules on Missile Exports," *Washington Post*, August 25,
2002.

stated "Beijing is believed to have an advanced chemical warfare program" and "China continues to maintain some elements of an offensive biological warfare program."[24]

In each of the case studies reviewed here there have been successes. However, the United States has had only limited influence over Chinese policies. In the case of military relations, U.S. influence through existing contacts appears to be extremely limited or nonexistent in crisis situations. Perhaps the overriding reason is because persons of influence in the PLA are political survivors who know how to read and react to government policy so their careers remain intact. During crisis situations it may be politically risky for these people to talk to the United States, closing existing lines of communication.

In the case of intellectual property rights, the United States has used a combination of economic incentives and disincentives to compel China to strengthen its IPR institutions and enforcement of IPR laws, yet China ultimately changed its policies only when it served its own self-interest. In the case of arms control and nonproliferation, China has joined many arms control and nonproliferation organizations under both U.S. and international pressure. In those areas in which the United States and China have signed bilateral agreements (such as missile nonproliferation), the United States has imposed a mix of economic and political incentives and disincentives to influence China's compliance behavior, including efforts to press China to accede to U.S. demands during times of renewed progress in the overall bilateral relationship. This suggests that China did not change its policies because of a commitment to the principles of nonproliferation but rather because of a reassessment of its own national interest, often in the pursuit of improvement in the overall bilateral relationship.

Consequently, there are three salient implications for the military relationship: China is more influenced by international opinion than by U.S. pressure alone; economic incentives and disincentives have had a measured success in changing Chinese behavior; and the

---

[24] U.S. Department of Defense, *Proliferation: Threat and Response*, January 2001, pp. 13–14.

military relationship does not exist in a vacuum but is shaped by the tenor and relative atmosphere of the overall political and diplomatic relationship.

Reciprocity and Transparency

Perhaps the most important issue is the current debate over reciprocity and transparency. The lack of reciprocity in the U.S.-China military relationship is universally acknowledged, even by the PLA. The PLA is widely believed to restrict the number and type of units that can be visited, repeatedly taking different delegations to the same units, including "showcase" units that do not accurately represent the true quality of PLA forces.

According to the 2002 *Annual Report on the Military Power of the People's Republic of China*, "since the 1980s, U.S. military exchange delegations to China have been shown only 'showcase units,' never any advanced units or any operational units."[25] PLA delegations, on the other hand, have been given access to numerous U.S. facilities of varying sensitivity. In addition, the openness, or transparency, of the PLA is also considered a problem—the PLA releases little information about itself during these visits.

The PLA gives several reasons for its lack of reciprocity and transparency. First, it argues that certain units are still backward and it is embarrassing to show their lack of capability. Second, the PLA sometimes claims that it is too poor and cannot carry out certain activities because of lack of funds.[26] The main obstacle, however, to improving reciprocity and transparency is the lack of mutual trust engendered by differing world visions, strategies, and actions. China perceives that the United States is treating it as a potential adversary. Because the PLA would be the weaker side in a military confrontation with the United States, it is reluctant to reveal its full capabilities to the U.S. military on the grounds that it would render itself more vul-

---

[25] U.S. Department of Defense, *Annual Report on the Military Power of the People's Republic of China*, July 12, 2002, p. 1.

[26] One PLA interlocutor asserted that most units do not have discretionary funds for entertaining foreign delegations.

nerable. Thus, the PLA finds it in its own interest to hide its capabilities. The U.S. military, on the other hand, has a surplus of strength that some believe can be openly displayed with little effect on the military's ability to fight wars. Because the United States, in part, wants to use military relations to deter China from taking actions that may negatively affect U.S. national interests, the United States has periodically determined that it is in its best interest to be open to the PLA.

Given the consensus that reciprocity and transparency are obstacles to the deepening of U.S.-China military relations, the debate has focused not on whether China is playing fair but rather on how to respond. Those who are more optimistic about changing Chinese behavior believe that only by continuing military contacts can the United States make the PLA more open. Also, some believe the United States has power and transparency to spare, and can therefore afford asymmetry. Others argue that because so much can be learned about the U.S. military through open sources and that so little is known about the PLA, the U.S. military has more to gain from exchanges, even if the flow of information is not equal. Still others argue that the reciprocity and transparency issues are partly a U.S. problem and that better preparation, coordination, and internal discipline in the military-to-military process can allow the U.S. military to improve the results of such exchanges. To solve the reciprocity problem, some suggest tailoring functional exchanges to maximize what the United States learns about the PLA. They fear that cutting off military relations with China or not conducting functional exchanges "could actually inhibit DoD's ability to learn more about China's military modernization efforts."[27] They believe "the best way to determine PLA's modernization effort is to talk with experts at multiple levels. This includes high-level discussions on strategic issues, as well as discussions on strategy, doctrine, and warfighting ca-

---

[27] Kenneth W. Allen, "U.S.-China Military Relations Not a One-Way Street," *Stimson Center News Advisory*, December 13, 1999, www.stimson.org/meida?sn-ME11221208.

pabilities by military operators."[28] Some may even suggest restarting arms sales as a way to improve or facilitate relations with the PLA.[29]

For others, however, the problems of reciprocity and transparency appear intractable. In their view, the American penchant for openness and the Chinese penchant for secrecy is a dangerous mix that facilitates the passage of potentially damaging information to the PLA. They point to circumstances in which PLA officers were allowed to tour nuclear submarines and joint warfighting facilities and were briefed on the conduct of military operations. This group believes that the transfer of intelligence or information to the PLA has helped China develop countermeasures to U.S. technology or counterstrategies to U.S. methods of warfare and that this know-how could be used against Taiwan and U.S. forces.

To assess the validity of these arguments, we looked at both quantifiable and qualitative data. According to information collected by the U.S. Department of Defense (see Table 4.1), U.S. delegations visited 51 different PLA units between 1993 and 1999.

In contrast, according to data in Table 4.2, the PLA made 137 visits to 73 different U.S. military units between 1994 and 1999. Thus, from a simple numerical standpoint, the PLA has visited more U.S. units. However, the claim by some in the United States that the PLA frequently takes U.S. delegations to the same units cannot be confirmed. Available data indicate only the years in which units were visited, not the frequency of unit visits within a particular year. However, all interlocutors indicate that this has been a continuing problem.

The statement in the DoD *Annual Report on the Military Power of the People's Republic of China* that the U.S. military has been shown only "showcase units" and has not visited any advanced units appears to be inaccurate. Some lesser-equipped units have been visited by U.S. military, such as the 179th and the 196th Infantry Divisions. The U.S. military has not visited China's Su-27 bases, but it has

---

[28] Allen, 1999.

[29] DoD News Briefing, January 20, 1998.

Table 4.1
Chinese Facilities Visited by U.S. Military Delegations

Number	Unit	Year
1	179th Infantry Division, Nanjing	1997, 1998
2	196th Infantry Division, Yangcun	1994, 1995, 1997
3	47th Group Army Hq, Xi'an	1998
4	6th Tank Division, Beijing	1996, 1997, 1998
5	3rd Garrison Division, Beijing	1998
6	Army Independent Regiment, Shenyang Military Region	1997
7	Tianjin Garrison Command	1998
8	PLA Academy of Military Science	1993, 1998
9	PLA National Defense University, Beijing	1993, 1994, 1995, 1996, 1997, 1998
10	PLA Academy of Military Medicine	1998
11	PLA Military Museum, Beijing	1997
12	PLA National Training Base, San Jie	1998
13	Chinese International Institute of Strategic Studies	1993, 1995
14	General Logistics Department Hq, Beijing	1997
15	General Logistics Department Mengtougou Fuel Depot	1997
16	General Logistics Department Mengtougou Vehicle Spare Parts Warehouse	1997
17	General Logistics Department Quartermaster Equipment Research Institute, Beijing	1997
18	General Logistics Department Command Academy	1997

Table 4.1 (continued)

Number	Unit	Year
19	Commission on Science, Technology, and Industry for National Defense (COSTIND) Hq	1994, 1997
20	COSTIND/General Armament Department Satellite Control Center, Xi'an	1993, 1994, 1996, 1997
21	Military Region Hq, Guangzhou	1997
22	Military Region Hq, Lanzhou	1997
23	Army Command Academy, Nanjing	1997, 1998
24	Army Academy, Dalian	1996, 1997
25	Army Academy, Guilin	1998
26	Army Armored Forces Engineering College, Beijing	1996
27	Army Artillery Academy, Nanjing	1997, 1998
28	Shenyang Ammunition Repairing and Testing Station	1997
29	Air Force Hq, Beijing	1996, 1999
30	Air Force Command College	1998
31	Air Force Beijing Air Defense Command Center	1998
32	Air Force Cangzhou Flight Test and Training Center	1997
33	Air Force Communications NCO[a] School	1999
34	Air Force Engineering College, Xi'an	1993
35	Air Force Radar College	1999
36	Air Force Base, Shijiazhuang	1999
37	Air Force 24th Air Wing, Yangcun	1994, 1995, 1996, 1997

Table 4.1 (continued)

Number	Unit	Year
38	Air Force 28th Bomber Division, Hangzhou	1998
39	Navy Hq, Beijing	1996
40	Air Force 15th Airborne Army, Airborne Unit, Kaifeng	1997
41	Air Force 4th Flying College	1999
42	Navy Command College, Nanjing	1995, 1999
43	Air Force 9th Air Division, Guangzhou, Foshan	1995, 1998
44	Navy Surface Warfare Academy, Dalian	1996, 1997
45	Navy Surface Warfare Academy, Guangzhou	1993, 1994, 1997, 1998
46	Navy South Sea Fleet Hq, Zhanjiang	1995
47	Navy 1st Marine Brigade, Zhanjiang	1997
48	Navy Base, Guangzhou	1997
49	Navy Base, Qingdao	1996
50	Navy Base, Shanghai	1995, 1998
51	Navy Base, Zhanjiang	1997

SOURCE: U.S. Department of Defense, *Report of Past Military to Military Exchanges and Contacts Between the U.S. and PRC.*
aNoncommissioned officer.

visited the 9th Air Division in Guangzhou, which bases the F-8II, a late model, domestically produced fighter that is the only air refuelable aircraft in the PLA inventory. Other units, perhaps not as advanced as U.S. units, are nevertheless considered frontline units in the PLA. For example, the 1st Marine Brigade is one of two active Marine brigades of the PLA. The Air Force Cangzhou Flight Test and Training Center is an active school with "three primary missions: to

Table 4.2
U.S. Facilities Visited by Chinese Military Delegations

Number	Unit	Times Visited	Years
1	National Defense University	10	1994, 1995 (4), 1996, 1997, 1998 (2), 1999
2	Armed Forces Staff College	1	1994
3	Naval Academy	1	1994
4	Air University	3	1995, 1996 (2)
5	Naval Air Station North Pointe, Point Loma	1	1995
6	Camp Pendleton	1	1995
7	Pacific Command	12	1994, 1995 (3), 1996 (3), 1997(3), 1998 (2)
8	U.S. Army Pacific Command	1	1995
9	Schofield Barracks	3	1995, 1996, 1998
10	U.S. Military Academy	8	1995, 1996, 1997 (3), 1998 (3)
11	U.S. Air Force Academy	3	1996, 1997, 1998
12	Citadel	1	1998
13	Asia Pacific Center for Security Studies	2	1996, 1997
14	U.S. Army Training and Doctrine Command	2	1997, 1998
15	Joint Training, Analysis, and Simulations Center	2	1998, 1999
16	Fort Leavenworth	2	1998
17	Atlantic Command	2	1997

Table 4.2 (continued)

Number	Unit	Times Visited	Years
18	Fort Bragg	3	1997 (2), 1998
19	Nellis AFB	4	1997(2), 1998, 199￼
20	Fort Irwin	1	1997
21	Air Force Satellite Control Network Command	2	1999 (2)
22	Kaneohe, Marine Corps Base	1	1998
23	Naval War College	2	1999
24	Fort Hood	3	1997, 1999, 2000
25	1st MEB	1	1994
26	PACAF	3	1994, 1995, 1997
27	Marine Forces Pacific	1	1998
28	USA Medical Research and Material Command	1	1995
29	Guam	1	1995
30	Tyndall AFB	1	1995
31	Maxwell AFB	2	1996
32	Davis-Monthan AFB	1	1995
33	Industrial College of the Armed Forces	2	1996, 1998
34	Army Material Command	1	1996
35	Defense Logistics Agency, Fort Belvoir	1	1996
36	ALMC[a] Satellite Education Network Center	1	1996

Table 4.2 (continued)

Number	Unit	Times Visited	Years
37	Fort Eustis Transportation School	2	1996, 1997
38	Langley Air Force Base	2	1996
39	Norfolk Naval Base	1	1996
40	Kelly AFB	1	1996
41	Pearl Harbor	6	1994, 1995 (2), 1996, 1997, 1998
42	Hickam AFB	3	1996, 1997, 1998
43	25th Infantry Division	1	1996
44	Air Command and Staff College	1	1996
45	Sandia National Laboratory	1	1996
46	Fort Monroe	1	1997
47	U.S. Army War College	2	1997, 1999
48	Fort Lewis	2	1997, 1998
49	Fort Shafter	2	1997, 1998
50	Camp Smith	1	1997
51	Marine Forces Pacific	1	1997
52	Commander, Naval Base, San Diego	1	1997
53	Atlantic Command	1	1997
54	Pacific Fleet	1	1997
55	Fort Knox	1	1997
56	Fort Campbell	1	1997

Table 4.2 (continued)

Number	Unit	Times Visited	Years
57	National Training Center	1	1997
58	Elmendorf AFB	2	1997, 1998
59	Fort Monmouth	1	1998
60	Fort Benning	2	1998 (2)
61	Fort Monroe	2	1998 (2)
62	Norfolk Naval Base	1	1998
63	Fort Lee	1	1998
64	USAF ROTC[b]	1	1998
65	Citadel	1	1998
66	Univ. of Colorado ROTC	1	1998
67	Princeton ROTC	1	1998
68	Aberdeen Proving Ground	1	1998
69	Warner Robbins Air Logistics Center	1	1998
70	Defense Logistics Agency Defense Supply Center	1	1998
71	Tripler Army Medical Center	1	1998
Total		137	

SOURCE: U.S. Department of Defense, *Report of Past Military to Military Exchanges and Contacts Between the U.S. and PRC.* Table 4.2 does not include PLA visits to the Pentagon or individual ships or units visited at a particular base. It does not include visits to nonmilitary organizations such as the White House, Department of Commerce, the Office of Management and Budget, the Federal Aviation Administration, Gettysburg National Military Park, and FedEx Headquarters.
[a]Army Logistics Management College.
[b]Reserve Officer Training Corps.

test new aircraft under development by the aviation ministry; to train the initial cadre of pilots in new type aircraft before the aircraft are deployed to an operational base for the first time; and to devise new air combat tactics."[30] Although not a unit equipped with advanced aircraft, the 28th Ground Attack Division was visited in 1998 and performed an ordnance loading and a live-fire demonstration by four A-5s.[31] The 28th Ground Attack Division is also one of China's lead ground-attack units.

The U.S. military, on the other hand, has shown the PLA elite units such as the 82nd Airborne Division at Fort Bragg, where they witnessed live-fire demonstrations and parachute drops. Although these were staged events, the PLA has also had access to unscripted training events, such as exercises at the National Training Center, Red Flag exercises, and a Marine Corps exercise. The U.S. military attended only one PLA exercise, in November 2000, but there is some debate over whether the exercise was staged. Regardless, the discrepancies in reciprocity and transparency point to the lack of U.S. access to unstaged or "real" exercises, as opposed to training carried out specifically for the U.S. military's benefit.

A second issue is the amount of information conveyed during these meetings or, more simply, what the delegations got out of the visit. This transparency issue must rely on a qualitative analysis. Once again, using data collected by the Office of the Secretary of Defense (OSD), it is possible to review the itineraries of PLA general and flag-grade officer visits and then compare the information with that provided by interlocutors on the types of itineraries provided to U.S. delegations. Of course, any such comparison lacks input from PLA participants about how they viewed the value of their visits to the United States.

---

[30] Kenneth Allen, "China's Aviation Capabilities," paper presented at Chinese Military Affairs: a Conference on the State of the Field, sponsored by the National Defense University, October 26–27, 2000.

[31] Brad Kaplan, "China and U.S.: Building Military Relations," *Asia-Pacific Defense Forum* (online), Summer 1999.

Most of the itineraries provided by OSD show a schedule full of different activities, from Pentagon visits, briefings, and unit visits to shopping and trips to Las Vegas. Chinese delegations have witnessed airborne operations and tank gunnery training, and have toured U.S. naval nuclear submarines and aircraft carriers, where they took part in an arrested landing and a catapult takeoff. The PLA has also received briefings on U.S. logistics, U.S. Army training and readiness, and joint training as well as individual unit or command briefs.

A look at several itineraries illustrates the types of activities PLA delegations took part in while in the United States. For example, the delegation of PLA Chief of General Staff General Fu Quanyou visited the United States August 3–13, 1997 and had a full schedule of activities that appear to be useful to the PLA.

3–4 August:	Tour New York city, courtesy of PRC UN Mission
5 August:	Tour West Point and Fort Bragg (live-fire demonstration, heavy drop rigging site demonstration)
6 August:	Tour Atlantic command (visit CVN); tour of Air Combat Command
7 August:	Meet with National Security Adviser Sandy Berger and Secretary of Defense William Cohen
8 August:	Meet with the chairman of the Joint Chiefs of Staff; Pentagon tour
9 August:	Tour Washington, D.C., travel to San Francisco
10 August:	Travel to Hawaii; meet with CINCPAC
11 August:	Meetings at PACOM

12 August: Meetings at PACOM, cultural touring

13 August: Return to China.[32]

A delegation led by Major General Dong Wancai in November 1998 included the following activities:

30 November: Visit Pentagon (meetings on officer accession and ROTC; meet with Deputy Chief of Staff for Personnel)

1 December: Visit Fort Monroe (meet with Assistant Deputy Chief of Staff for Base Operation Support, U.S. Army Training Command; Cadet Command briefing)

2 December: Visit Fort Bragg (meet with ROTC Region Chief of Staff and 5th Brigade Commander; visit Campbell University ROTC detachment)

3 December: Visit University of South Carolina ROTC detachment

4 December: Visit Citadel

5 December: Cultural tour

6 December: Tour USAF Academy

7 December: Tour USAF Academy (mission brief)

8 December: Visit USAF NW ROTC Region Headquarters; visit University of Colorado AF ROTC detachment

9 December: Visit University of Colorado ROTC prograr

[32] U.S. Department of Defense, *Report of Past Military to Military Exchanges and Contacts Between the U.S. and PRC.*

10 December: Visit Princeton ROTC detachment

11 December: Visit West Point

12 December: Depart for China.[33]

From the itineraries, it is apparent that useful information could have been conveyed to the PLA delegations during these trips. Although determining how much information was communicated and absorbed is difficult, an environment was created in which exchanges could take place.

Determining whether unit visits provided by the U.S. military are qualitatively better than those provided by the PLA is difficult. At various times both sides have expressed displeasure with functional visits. On the U.S. side, however, there is a widespread perception that the PLA withholds more information than does the U.S. military. For example, the PLA will give approximate numbers of personnel and equipment in briefings rather than the exact numbers typically provided by the U.S. military. In addition, PLA officers from the Foreign Affairs Office monitor such briefings, causing PLA briefers to be more restrictive in what they reveal to U.S. participants. Secrecy, in fact, is difficult to overcome. Occasionally, getting even the most basic information from PLA members is a challenge. During a PLA delegation visit to the United States in 1997, for example, delegation members refused to answer simple questions of unit designation, type of aircraft flown, or even what province they were from.[34] Thus, the nontransparent nature of the PLA affects even the most basic aspects of military-to-military activities and illustrates the difficulty the United States may have in achieving transparency.

---

[33] U.S. Department of Defense, *Report of Past Military to Military Exchanges and Contacts Between the U.S. and PRC.*

[34] U.S. Department of Defense, *Report of Past Military to Military Exchanges and Contacts Between the U.S. and PRC.*

Poor Planning Leads to Poor Performance

Chinese intransigence to opening up is just one part of the problem in military relations. Interlocutors familiar with past military-to-military activities point out that some of the blame for the perceived disparity in the value of military relations can be attributed to inefficiencies within the U.S. Defense Department. Systemic inefficiencies in the planning, execution, debriefing, and analysis of military-to-military activities with the PLA affect reciprocity and transparency in two ways. First, inefficiency hinders proper planning of trips to maximize benefit to the U.S. military. Second, it hinders the processing of information collected by military-to-military activities. Thus, the U.S. system has created an environment in which PLA openness may not have been recognized or exploited.

Pre-trip planning, for example, has been incomplete at times. In many instances, participants have been poorly briefed on the overall bilateral relationship and the role of military-to-military activities within the relationship, are given little or no background information on the topic or the personalities they will deal with, and are not properly briefed on the goals of the trip. Based on information collected by OSD, it also appears that gathering information on the PLA was not an explicit priority of the U.S. military during certain interactions. For example, information concerning the visit of PLA Deputy Chief of Staff Lt. General Wu Quanxu July 8–17, 1997 states that "the goals of the PLA for the visit are to establish counterpart relationship with USCINCPAC; understand more about U.S. methods for joint organization; learn more about U.S. training doctrine and procedures."[35] U.S. Commander in Charge, Pacific (USCINCPAC), goals for the visit, however, were to "establish personal relationships with key PLA military leaders; demonstrate USCINCPAC responsibility, military prowess, and professionalism" by providing Lt. General Wu with a "better understanding of USCINCPAC mission, organization and strategy and a better understanding of U.S. joint and service training doctrine and procedures; exchange views on military

---

[35] U.S. Department of Defense, *Report of Past Military to Military Exchanges and Contacts Between the U.S. and PRC.*

relations and contacts between USCINCPAC and the PLA; and expose Lt. General Wu and his delegation to American society and culture."[36] Thus, for this particular visit the goals of the U.S. military were influence-building, deterrence, and assisting the PLA to better understand the U.S. military. Increased understanding of the PLA, however, was not a goal. The difference in the goals can be attributed to the PLA making a trip to the United States to learn about the U.S. military. The fact that the U.S. military did not have an explicit goal to use this opportunity to learn more about the PLA, however, indicates that collecting information on the PLA, and hence making the PLA more transparent, was not a primary factor in at least some functional activities. Similarly, interviews suggest that U.S. military delegations to China are ill prepared to exploit opportunities for gathering information on the PLA simply because they are not briefed about what questions to ask. Proper briefings and knowing which questions to ask may go a long way toward increasing the absorption of information by delegations.

Another factor that inhibits PLA openness is that U.S. delegations repeatedly visit the same bases. U.S. delegations go to the same units or bases because the delegations frequently travel to the same cities and are in China for limited periods of time. For example, delegations often travel to Beijing, and time restrictions only allow visits to units within convenient traveling distance. Other bases are visited because of their proximity to tourist locations such as the Great Wall near Beijing or the terracotta warriors near Xi'an. By scheduling only enough time to visit units near major cities or tourist sites, the United States misses opportunities for wider knowledge of the PLA. The PLA compounds the U.S. military's lack of coordination by dealing with delegations on an individual basis—different delegations are composed of different participants who may not have seen a certain unit or base resulting in the same bases being visited multiple times.

One aspect of trip planning is determining who will take part in the delegation. In the past, high-level officers who were nearing re-

---

[36] U.S. Department of Defense, *Report of Past Military to Military Exchanges and Contacts Between the U.S. and PRC.*

tirement made trips to China. From the U.S. perspective, any benefit from these trips is lost when the officer retires in the months following the trip, although better post-trip debriefing could preserve most of the knowledge (see below). From the PLA perspective, there is little incentive to prepare an expansive itinerary when planners know the long-term value of the contact is extremely limited.

Finally, in the past the pace of the military relationship has affected the ability of the U.S. Defense Department to adequately plan itineraries. Increasing numbers of delegations traveling to China stretched the ability of the limited staffs of both OSD and the attaché office in Beijing to provide comprehensive trip planning.

In addition to trip planning, trip execution has at times been less than optimal. Delegations may not ask hard questions because they do not want to offend their Chinese hosts by appearing to prompt a classified response. Conversations between Americans and Chinese have been stifled for the simple reason that during meal times the Americans and Chinese sit at different tables. On other occasions, general and flag-grade officers have given unclassified reports to the PLA. Although it is preferred practice to give U.S. Defense Department publications in exchange for PLA publications, these officers, ignoring the advice of their subordinates, give the publications away, getting nothing in return.[37]

Debriefing, the third stage of managing military-to-military activities, has also been inadequate. Delegations have often not been debriefed or asked to write reports about their trips. In such cases, no institutional memory is preserved. This sharply contrasts with the Chinese side's legendary proclivity for record keeping. Moreover, even if a trip report is written, it is sometimes submitted only into service rather than intelligence channels. Wider dissemination of the information should be available to all potential interlocutors with the Chinese.

---

[37] Stephen J. Yates, Al Santoli, Randy Schriver, and Larry Wortzel, "The Proper Scope, Purpose, and Utility of U.S. Relations with China's Military," *Heritage Lectures*, October 10, 2000, p. 8 (for example).

A fourth aspect of military-to-military relations, post-trip analysis of the interactions and derived intelligence is as valuable as any of the other stages. Interlocutors assert that information from delegations often cannot be fully analyzed because of an inadequate number of qualified China analysts within the U.S. government.

Conclusion

In this chapter we have reviewed the arguments concerning the benefits of a military relationship with China, the potential harm to U.S. national security deriving from the military relationship, the ability of the United States to influence China, and the issues of reciprocity and transparency. The evidence from this review suggests that the United States has benefited from its military relationship with China, but it has also been harmed to a limited extent. The evidence also suggests that the ability of the United States to influence China through the military relationship will be highly circumscribed without an improvement in the overall bilateral relationship.

Analysis of the reciprocity and transparency issues reveals that the U.S. military has provided the PLA access to more units than has the PLA and that this access has been of higher value. All interlocutors state that the PLA repeatedly takes U.S. delegations to the same units and that the content of these visits is much less specific and informative than the content of briefings and demonstrations given to the PLA. In addition, while the PLA has not taken the U.S. military to its most advanced units, such as Su-27 bases, the assertion that the U.S. military has only been shown showcase units and has not seen the PLA's advanced units is not accurate. Thus, the discrepancy over reciprocity and transparency does not so much revolve around the types of bases visited and the frequency of visits as it does around the U.S. military not being shown operational training or realistic exercises, to which the PLA has had access, and to the content of functional visits.

Resolving problems on the Chinese side, however, will not completely solve the reciprocity and transparency issues. Systemic problems within the Defense Department have also lowered the value of military-to-military contacts. Better coordination, planning, exploitation, and documentation may be able to ameliorate some of the effects of PLA intransigence.

CHAPTER FIVE

Chinese Views of Military Relationships

To accurately assess the U.S.-China military relationship, it is necessary to consider not only the debate within the United States but also Chinese views on establishing and maintaining cooperative relationships. This chapter assesses the reasons why Beijing conducts military relations and then reviews Chinese perceptions of military relations with the United States.

According to a study by the Center for Naval Analyses (CNA), the PLA conducts foreign military relations to "help shape the international security environment in support of key national security objectives. Two of those key security objectives are the modernization of the Chinese state and the defense and pursuit of Chinese sovereignty."[1] To sustain its modernization drive, Chinese officials insist that Beijing must maintain a peaceful and stable regional security environment. To this end, China's military relations must prevent armed conflict with potential adversaries and strengthen relationships with friends. As the Center for Naval Analyses notes:

> To a large degree, then, because China belongs to no formal alliances, and in fact eschews them, PLA foreign military relations can generally be characterized as serving preemptive purposes

---

[1] David M. Finkelstein and John Unangst, *Engaging DoD: Chinese Perspectives on Military Relations with the United States*, Alexandria, VA: Center for Naval Analyses Corporation, October 1999, p. 5.

rather than serving as a vehicle for inclusiveness or coalition building against common threats.[2]

The most important Chinese objective for military relations is to defend national sovereignty. China's principal sovereignty issue is Taiwan, but it also has disagreements with Japan over the Diaoyu/Senkaku islands, with Vietnam over the demarcation of the Gulf of Tonkin, and with various Southeast Asian countries over areas of the South China Sea. In an effort to persuade the United States not to support Taiwan, Beijing regularly states its position that Taiwan is a part of China and that it does not renounce the right to use force to reclaim Taiwan. To other countries, such as those in Southeast Asia, it is decidedly less provocative. In both Track 1 and Track 2 venues, China has been emphasizing diplomacy rather than military force in sovereignty claims as a way to dispel notions that China is a threat.[3]

As CNA observes, "China's foreign military relations are also expected to contribute to the ongoing modernization of the PLA and the Chinese defense establishment."[4] Most obvious are Chinese purchases of Russian military equipment such as submarines and fighter aircraft. But perhaps more important are improvements in "software." Foreign military relations allow opportunities for PLA officers to

- stay abreast of the changes in modern warfare;
- acquire modern military knowledge in doctrine, operations, training, administration, and the entire gamut of combat support and combat service support operations;
- train military and PLA civil cadre technicians and specialists;
- broaden younger officers by sending them abroad;
- expose senior officers to military developments in more technologically advanced countries; and

---

[2] Finkelstein and Unangst, p. 6.

[3] Finkelstein and Unangst, p. 7.

[4] Finkelstein and Unangst, p. 9.

- advance key PLA R&D programs by soliciting foreign assistance.[5]

Chinese foreign military relations also have a larger political component usually reflecting the state of the overall bilateral relationship with that country. China can advance or reverse a bilateral relationship, in part, by increasing or reducing its military ties with that country.[6] Accordingly, "the PLA's foreign military relations are primarily strategic activities, expected to support broader national security objectives and the PLA's key national military objectives."[7]

China's overall objectives in pursuing foreign military relations are reflected in its dealings with the U.S. military. The relationship with the DoD, however, is probably the most significant relationship for the PLA because of the challenges the United States poses to some of China's core security concerns. Washington is the main provider of military equipment to Taipei and has made clear its intention to come to the defense of Taiwan if that country is attacked without provocation. In addition, the military presence of the United States in Asia, especially in South Korea and Japan, influences Chinese security concerns. U.S. "soft power" can also influence China's interests in Asia through diplomacy and economics.

All of these concerns indicate that the PLA must manage, if not resolve, issues with the United States that could turn into conflict. As stated above, a key security objective is the modernization of the Chinese state. Consequently, China must maintain a peaceful and stable regional security environment to achieve continued economic development. A principal factor in China's economic modernization drive is continued trade with the United States. According to Chinese government statistics, the United States is China's second largest

---

[5] Finkelstein and Unangst, p. 9.

[6] Finkelstein and Unangst, p. 11.

[7] Finkelstein and Unangst, p. 12.

trading partner (behind Japan) and its largest export market.[8] China must therefore seek to avoid diplomatic and military conflicts that could jeopardize its economic relationship with the United States. Conflict avoidance, the most important goal for the PLA in its relations with the U.S. military, is carried out in two ways. In nearly all venues, the Chinese will reiterate their view that Taiwan is the paramount issue in U.S.-China relations and that it must be "carefully managed." They will also remind their U.S. counterparts that China will not give up the right to use force to unify Taiwan with the mainland. At the same time, the PLA will also use every opportunity to try to refute the "China threat theory." The Chinese assert that their

> strategic intentions do not pose a military threat to any nation and that the PLA is a relatively backward force that cannot pose a major threat to any nation, certainly not the United States. . . . In short, the PLA uses the military relationship to attempt to affect U.S. attitudes. Every facet of the military relationship is used to prompt dialogues in which the PLA can state its case.[9]

The military-to-military relationship cannot be divorced from the overall bilateral relationship with the United States. In the past, agreements with the United States have been made to advance the overall bilateral relationship, not because China believed the agreements were valuable in and of themselves. For example, the MMCA had been proposed by the United States in 1995, but the Chinese did not agree to it in principle until the presidential summit in October 1997. It was not signed until Secretary of Defense Cohen visited Beijing in 1998. Similarly, the U.S. proposal for a series of reciprocal briefings on humanitarian assistance/disaster relief, which was to culminate in a sand-table exercise, was also agreed upon in principle during the 1997 presidential summit.[10] In both cases, these activities

---

[8] "Facts and Figures: China's Top Ten Trade Partners in 2001," *People's Daily* (online), February 13, 2002.

[9] Finkelstein and Unangst, p. 28.

[10] Finkelstein and Unangst, pp. 24–25.

were agreed to because the United States desired summit deliverables and not because the Chinese agreed in principle they were of value.

As discussed in the previous chapter, a secondary goal of the PLA's military relationship with the United States is to support defense modernization. According to CNA, "The PLA uses functional and professional exchanges to learn as much as it can from the U.S. defense establishment to support China's military modernization and reform program."[11] Because the United States maintains the most advanced military in the world, "PLA military professionals are eager to learn whatever they can from the U.S. defense establishment."[12]

The U.S.-China military relationship aids PLA modernization in three primary ways, according to Chinese interlocutors. First, as stated above, the United States has the most advanced military in the world. By learning about U.S. military capabilities, the PLA can establish benchmarks by which it can assess its own modernization efforts. Second, the PLA can learn how U.S. operations are conducted as well as the requirements and limitations of U.S. equipment. This can help China determine how the United States might operate in a conflict with China and provide insights into how the PLA should conduct its own operations. Third, exposing PLA personnel to the U.S. military helps "break down internal resistance to the sweeping, and often painful, military reform programs that are currently underway in the Chinese military."[13] PLA streamlining has broken "iron rice bowls"[14] that have existed for decades. Allowing PLA personnel to witness the U.S. military has provided ample evidence for the need to make painful reforms.

China would also like to receive U.S. military technology. However, the PLA realizes "that the United States is not going to provide

---

[11] Finkelstein and Unangst, p. 30.

[12] Finkelstein and Unangst, p. 30.

[13] Finkelstein and Unangst, p. 30.

[14] *Tie fanwan* in Chinese. Iron rice bowl refers to the all-encompassing cradle-to-grave support that the Chinese government used to give its citizens.

either dual-use technologies or military end items."[15] The PLA does continue to press for a lifting of the Tiananmen sanctions so that spare parts for the Black Hawk helicopters sold to it in the 1980s can be acquired. One recent justification given by the PLA for the sale of the spare parts is to enable the PLA to better conduct search and rescue missions for U.S. pilots should any crash in China while conducting operations in support of Operation Enduring Freedom.[16]

The willingness of the United States to conduct functional and professional exchanges (FPE) with the PLA and transfer military technology to China is also valued for its political symbolism. In fact,

> the degree to which the United States will accommodate the PLA's requests for exposure to high-tech U.S. capabilities through FPEs and whether any cracks in the Tiananmen sanctions can be breached are two measures used by the PLA to gauge whether the United States considers China a potential enemy.[17]

The Chinese Approach to Military Relations

The Chinese approach to military relations is fundamentally different from the U.S. approach. The U.S. approach assumes that operational-level activities can lead to understanding and trust at a strategic level. Taking military relations as an example, a common U.S. approach would be to engage in functional exchanges so that personal relationships can be developed between individual officers and points of convergence or commonality of purpose can be identified. By working in identified areas of agreement, more trust can be built upon which a foundation for a strategic framework can be laid.

---

[15] Finkelstein and Unangst, p. 30.

[16] Interview, June 2002.

[17] Finkelstein and Unangst, p. 30.

The Chinese, on the other hand, prefer to begin with strategic-level dialogue to achieve mutual understanding through agreement on common principles, building trust from the top-down. As CNA observes, "In theory, each side must be willing to frankly confront strategic differences, take each other's concerns on-board, and commit to finding either resolution or an appropriate *modus vivendi.*"[18] Resolution of differences can then lead to mutual trust. Only after mutual trust is achieved can cooperative activities begin at lower levels. Thus, in the Chinese construct, cooperation is the result of mutual trust whereas cooperation in the American construct is a pathway to build trust.[19]

What does this construct mean for the way in which the PLA conducts its military relations with the United States? If a measure of trust is achieved, the PLA appears to be willing to engage in more forward-leaning activities, such as the nuclear de-targeting agreement and functional exchanges. Without a resolution of strategic issues, the PLA is likely to be comfortable only with high-level exchanges such as the DCTs and the NDU-to-NDU relationship. However, without a resolution of strategic issues, moving from strategic dialogue to cooperative activities with the PLA may be difficult. CNA concludes:

> Consequently, the degree to which the PLA will be willing to engage in operational activities with the U.S. defense establishment depends on Beijing's assessment of strategic understanding at any given time, or put, alternatively, the willingness of the United States to make concessions on issues important to Beijing.[20]

This was exemplified by the agreements on sand-table exercises for humanitarian assistance/disaster relief and the MMCA. What appears to have made these agreements possible is "a political calculus that the overall benefits to China from the 1997 and 1998 presidential sum-

---

[18] Finkelstein and Unangst, p. 17.

[19] Finkelstein and Unangst, p. 18.

[20] Finkelstein and Unangst, p. 19.

mits justified having the PLA engage in mechanisms with DoD that it otherwise was reluctant to sign up to."[21] Thus, these agreements were not signed because the PLA believed mutual trust had been achieved; rather, Beijing took the entire relationship into consideration before authorizing these contacts.

Implications

China's views of its military relationship with the United States and the way in which decisions on military relations are made have important implications for the U.S. military. First, without progress or the hope of progress in the overall relationship, it may be difficult to achieve agreement on cooperative military activities. The value of a program will be recognized only in relation to the overall bilateral relationship.

Second, this inherently political view of the military relationship has meant that at times the PLA has been directed against its will to participate with the U.S. military. During the late 1990s, Party leaders decided to engage the United States at all levels and directed the PLA to take part in cooperative activities even though the PLA was reluctant. The consequence of this type of decisionmaking is that

> while the top political leadership can impose a mil-to-mil requirement on a reluctant PLA, how that activity with the United States is executed is left to the PLA. Even after the political decision to go ahead has been made the PLA can drag their feet and make actual execution very difficult. Consequently, agreements in principle may not necessarily translate into expected action "on the ground."[22]

PLA distrust of military cooperation with the United States is partially a consequence of explicit U.S. goals of deterrence, intelligence gathering, and influence. Washington conducts military rela-

---

[21] Finkelstein and Unangst, p. 19.

[22] Finkelstein and Unangst, p. 32.

tions to deter Beijing from engaging in actions that could bring it into armed conflict with the United States and to gather intelligence on the Chinese military. Finally, the United States uses the military relationship to "influence the thinking and views of the PLA to achieve U.S. security objectives and change the nature of the political system. This latter point, changing the Chinese political system, is seen as particularly loathsome" by the Chinese.[23] From these objectives, the Chinese conclude that the purpose of the United States in pursuing military relations with China is inherently hostile.[24]

The combination of lack of mutual trust and the reluctance of the PLA to participate with the U.S. military in cooperative activities explains the continuing inability to achieve reciprocity and transparency. First, although progress in the overall bilateral relationship may have led to agreements, the PLA's fundamental lack of trust of the United States may have hampered the proper execution of these agreements. Second, just as the United States has used Chinese visits to affect PLA perceptions, China has used U.S. visits to affect U.S. military perceptions. To refute the "China threat theory," the PLA has carefully controlled "what U.S. military officials are permitted to see of the operational PLA, so the on the ground impression gained by visitors supports its case."[25]

However, the underlying obstacle to genuine reciprocity lies in the differences in strategic intent between the two countries. The United States views China with ambivalence. From Washington's point of view, China's increasing military and economic power could be used against U.S. national interests. To ensure that China does not miscalculate and start a military conflict involving the United States, Washington has a strategic interest in being very open to the PLA about its military prowess in order to deter China. Conversely, Beijing is also suspicious of Washington's strategic intentions. U.S. assistance to Taiwan, reconnaissance flights off China's coast, research

---

[23] Finkelstein and Unangst, p. 37.

[24] Finkelstein and Unangst, p. 36.

[25] Finkelstein and Unangst, p. 28.

into missile defenses, the bombing of the Chinese embassy in Belgrade, and the perceived "encirclement" of the PRC by U.S. forces in support of the war on terror all signal to Beijing that Washington may be trying to contain it. Because it is a weaker power than the United States, China believes its strategic interest lies in hiding its capability. Thus, the Chinese perception is that openness helps the United States and hurts China. In the words of one senior Chinese military official, "transparency is a tool of the strong to be used against the weak."[26]

The PLA is also reportedly "well aware that the U.S. defense establishment is dissatisfied with China's level of defense transparency."[27] However, the Chinese would likely counter that the U.S. Defense Department is not in turn totally transparent in its dealings with the PLA. They point to the U.S. military denying PLA access to facilities and refusing to discuss certain issues or permit the sale of dual-use technologies to China.[28] In addition, the Chinese are keenly aware that the United States employs openness as a tool of deterrence, which is viewed as a threat by some in the PLA. One Chinese official has stated:

> For the U.S. side transparency means deterrence. Some of your people are too arrogant. The United States says the PLA needs to see more U.S. capabilities in order to scare them. When the U.S. side talks like that why should China do anything to build confidence with the U.S.?[29]

In this case, the United States can be said to want transparency at the operational level whereas China wants transparency at the strategic level.[30] Thus, until China is comfortable with U.S. strategic intentions, significant obstacles to reciprocity will continue to exist.

---

[26] Interview, Beijing, January 2001.

[27] Finkelstein and Unangst, p. 41.

[28] Finkelstein and Unangst, pp. 42–43.

[29] Finkelstein and Unangst, p. 42.

[30] Finkelstein and Unangst, p. 41.

This begs the question of what the United States can do to make China more comfortable with U.S. strategic intentions. Finkelstein and Unangst outline some actions Beijing suggests the United States could take to ameliorate Chinese concerns:

- Share important strategic information that affects Beijing's interests, such as U.S. intentions regarding North Korea
- Discuss U.S. military contingency plans for the Korean peninsula
- Hold dialogues with the PLA on the "proper security role" of Japan in Asia
- Curtail and eventually cease arms sales to Taiwan
- Lift technology sanctions against the PLA
- Allow a wider range of discussion on professional military issues such as the RMA and logistics.[31]

Each of these actions, however, is problematic for the United States. Sharing strategic information on issues affecting China, such as Korea, may be foolhardy, because China could be a future adversary. Similarly, discussing military contingency plans for operations against North Korea could provide vital information to a country that has described its relationship with North Korea as that "between lips and teeth" and thus risk American and allied lives. The Chinese desire to hold dialogues on the "proper security role" of Japan in Asia hints that the Chinese view Japan as a threat to Asia. The United States, on the other hand, would like the Japanese military to be less restricted in its operations. Curtailing and eventually ceasing arms sales to Taiwan would violate the spirit of the Taiwan Relations Act, call into question the U.S. commitment to support its friends and allies, and sow doubt about America's commitment to support democracy. Finally, lifting technology sanctions against the PLA or allowing a wider range of discussion on professional military issues could improve the PLA's ability to conduct combat operations, possi-

---

[31] Finkelstein and Unangst, pp. 34–35.

bly against the United States or Taiwan. Thus, it appears that the United States is precluded from taking the very actions that could potentially increase mutual trust with China and thereby improve the chances for full Chinese cooperation in military-to-military activities.

CHAPTER SIX

Conclusion and Recommendations[1]

The previous U.S. Department of Defense restrictions on military-to-military relations with China stirred a debate about the proper role of those relations in overall U.S.-China relations and the wisdom of certain types of military-to-military activities. Under the restrictions, all official military-to-military activities, even U.S. military officers attending events hosted by third parties in which the PLA would be present, were approved by OSD on a case-by-case basis. The restrictions on military-to-military activities with the PLA were viewed as draconian by many, but in one sense they were valuable, reflecting the sensible approach of establishing a foundation for a policy before that policy was enacted.

Military Relations with the PLA: Worth the Trouble?

As argued in previous chapters, not only is there value in conducting some military-to-military activities with the PLA, but not doing so may actually increase chances of miscalculation and misperception that could lead to conflict. To illustrate with an extreme example, cutting off all military-to-military ties with the PLA would send a signal to the Chinese leadership that, at a minimum, the United

---

[1] Much of the information in this chapter is derived from interviews with people who have studied or been intimately involved in the U.S.-China military-to-military relationship. All prefer to remain anonymous.

States considers its relationship with China to be of diminished value. At a maximum, it could be interpreted as another signal that the United States considers China to be an enemy, leading China to take actions not in the interests of the United States. Cutting off all ties would eliminate lines of communication between the two militaries and increase the chances of misperception and miscalculation by not allowing either the U.S. military or the PLA to state their respective concerns and policies. Hearing the U.S. military voice how it might carry out operations against China in the event of armed conflict, for example, may influence the PLA differently than if they heard it from another U.S. government organization.

At the operational level, a hypothetical closing of the attaché office in China or heavily restricting the activities of the attachés would diminish the ability of the U.S. military to collect intelligence information. In addition, U.S. military officers who visit China from the National War College and NDU would not have an opportunity to experience China for themselves, possibly limiting their understanding of Asian security issues as they rise to higher policy-oriented positions. Not supporting Track 2 efforts or denying permission for government-funded researchers to have contacts with the Chinese would further inhibit understanding of China and the PLA. Often these activities can reveal areas of agreement that may be more difficult to uncover in an official setting. Ceasing functional exchanges may eliminate a potential source of information about the PLA (assuming of course, that functional exchanges can be properly conducted).

Designing an Effective Military Relationship with China

Constraints and Limitations

The two main constraints on conducting military-to-military relations with China are geostrategic and legal. The geostrategic environment, reviewed in Chapter Three, has changed from the 1980s, when the U.S.-China military relationship was at its most robust. Today, the relationship is mired in distrust caused by mutual suspicions of strategic intentions, accidents, and disagreements over Taiwan. These suspicions have led each country to regard the other as a strategic competitor and potential enemy. This situation has especially manifested itself in each country's Taiwan policies. The United States both in rhetoric and in substance is increasing support for Taiwan, whereas China increases its buildup of missiles opposite of Taiwan and its purchases of advanced Russian equipment. The potential for a conflict over Taiwan would seem to limit or prohibit certain kinds of military activities on the grounds that these activities could be used to improve the PLA so it can more effectively use force against Taiwan and the United States. Consequently, conducting the types of military-to-military activities with China that are conducted with friends and allies would be inappropriate. These activities include transferring arms or military-related technology and requesting basing, access, and overflights to conduct or support combat operations. Requesting overflights for humanitarian missions may be more acceptable.

The ambivalent nature of U.S.-China relations also affects the conduct of military relations. As reviewed in Chapter Four, the Chinese approach to conducting military relations is in polar opposition to the way in which the United States prefers to conduct military relations. In short, the Chinese prefer a top-down approach that requires agreement on or resolution of strategic issues that then must lead to the creation of mutual trust before cooperative activities can take place. The United States, on the other hand, prefers a bottom-up approach that emphasizes building trust at lower levels that can then be leveraged to find agreement on strategic issues. Without mutual trust in a relationship, the PLA will be uncomfortable with or not willing to engage in cooperative activities that would seem of value to the United States. In the past, this has resulted in a refusal to take part in certain activities as well as poor implementation of agreed-upon activities.

Legally, the United States is constrained by the 2000 National Defense Authorization Act, which forbids any

> military-to-military exchange or contact that would create a national security risk due to an inappropriate exposure to the PLA in the areas of force projection operations, nuclear operations, advanced logistical operations, chemical and biological defense and other capabilities related to weapons of mass destruction, surveillance and reconnaissance operations, joint warfighting experiments and other activities related to a transformation in warfare, military space operations, other advanced capabilities of the Armed Forces, arms sales or military-related technology transfers, release of classified or restricted information.[2]

Search and rescue and humanitarian operations and exercises are excluded from this restriction. Because in the current geopolitical situation China is a potential peer competitor of the United States, these restrictions rule out arms sales and military-related technology transfers. Such transfers could improve the PLA and enable it to better conduct combat operations against Taiwan and U.S. military forces, even while improving China's participation in the war on terror.

Another problem is the limited ability of the United States to influence China. As discussed in Chapter Three, the United States government has had few successes in influencing China and has had persistent failures in its attempts to use influence in the military-to-military context. Where the United States has had success it has relied primarily on economic incentives and disincentives, which may be inappropriate tools to use in the military-to-military context. Thus, a military relations program that posits influencing China as a main goal will probably not be successful.

Program of "Security Management"
A wide variety of military-to-military activities with the PLA has been carried out in the past with varying degrees of success. The constraints and limitations imposed upon the U.S. military relationship with China do present challenges for devising an effective program. However, any program must have an explicit set of goals, without

---

[2] U.S. Department of Defense, *Report of Past Military to Military Exchanges and Contacts Between the U.S. and PRC.*

which no program can be properly planned or evaluated. Based on the nature of the U.S.-China relationship, and the constraints imposed by both sides on the military-to-military relationship, the goals of a military relationship with China should be modest and achievable and should take into account not only U.S. concerns, but also the concerns and perceptions of the PLA. The ambivalent nature of the relationship also suggests that the United States should pursue a program of *security management* with China rather than a program of security cooperation. In security cooperation, militaries work together to promote common security against potential enemies. The goal of security management, in contrast, is to protect national security by reducing the chances of armed conflict between two countries, ensuring victory in case armed conflict does occur, and cooperating when appropriate against third-party threats, such as terrorism. Thus, the reasons for carrying out military-to-military activities with China will be different from those that are carried out with friends and allies. To address the challenges of the U.S.-China relationship, a program of security management with China should have three aspects: communication, information gathering, and limited cooperation.

Communication. Communication, broadly defined, can serve a useful purpose in U.S.-China military relations by providing a mechanism to avoid armed conflict. Communication can be conducted by both sides in pursuit of their national interests. For our purposes here, however, we examine how the U.S. Defense Department should communicate.

The U.S. military can communicate with the PLA in several ways. The first, dialogue—especially high-level dialogue—provides a forum where senior defense and military officials can communicate policy and intentions, identify and build upon areas of agreement, and resolve areas of disagreement. Dialogue can clear up misperceptions or clarify positions. For example, the United States military may need to explain U.S. government policies toward Taiwan. In addition, because some in China view the newly revised Nuclear Posture Review as directing the United States to use or at least threaten the use of nuclear weapons during a conflict over Taiwan, the U.S. military could use dialogue to better explain the logic behind the document. Dialogue can disabuse the PLA of incorrect thinking or conspiracy theories. According to many interlocutors, the PLA's Second Department, also known as the *erbu*, the organization responsible for collecting military intelligence, is notoriously bad at analyzing U.S. policy and has been known to provide politically correct recommendations. High-level talks could counter inaccurate analysis by the PLA by providing a direct communication link with top U.S. decisionmakers.

Dialogue with the PLA can also signal other countries that the United States is managing relations with China well and is taking steps to minimize the potential for conflicts. In this sense, U.S.-China military relations assure allies that the United States is doing its utmost to ensure peace and stability in Asia.

Dialogue can be used to deter China by having high-level military and Defense Department officials state that if called upon to defend Taiwan, the U.S. military will prosecute and win an armed conflict against China. Deterrence has also been communicated through actions, instead of words, but communicating deterrence, as with any attempt to influence China, has its limits. In the past, the U.S. military has attempted to deter China from taking actions counter to U.S. interests by showing U.S. capability to the PLA, as when PLA officers were flown over rows of M1A1 tanks at Fort Hood, Texas. There has been some debate whether such overt attempts at deterrence are necessary, considering that the U.S. performance in combat operations has done a better job of displaying U.S. military might than any forum or unit visit could do. Certainly, the U.S. military has impressed the PLA. Chinese writings are full of articles expressing admiration and awe for recent U.S. military performances. Yet the PLA still seems to look for ways to inflict casualties on the United States to make Washington lose the political will to assist Taiwan.[3] By this reasoning, China can use its military to achieve political effects and does not necessarily have to achieve a military victory

---

[3] See, for example, Jiang Lei, *Xiandai yilie shengyou zhanlue* [Modern Strategy of Using the Inferior to Defeat the Superior], Chinese Military Science Ph.D. Dissertation Series, National Defense University, 1997, pp. 117–188.

against the United States. In this case, deterrence may not work because China does not have to win; it just has to inflict enough casualties on the United States. It may then be essential for U.S. political leaders, both from the White House and Congress, as well as senior military and defense officials, to use dialogue to consistently reiterate U.S. interests and commitments regarding Taiwan in order to demonstrate U.S. political will. At the same time, heavy-handed attempts at deterrence may have unintended negative consequences, driving the PLA to backpedal on agreed military-to-military activities. By some accounts, the PLA understands the deterrence message given during these types of activities and resents it.

Dialogue also fits nicely with the Chinese view of conducting bilateral relationships. The Chinese see dialogue as a confidence-building measure and, in fact, have stated in the past that high-level dialogues have been too short and too infrequent.[4] Holding high-level talks would serve both countries' interests. The United States would have an opportunity to conduct talks in support of its goals. China would be able to operate in a comfortable venue in which it would have an opportunity to work toward mutual understanding that could then be used to develop mutual trust. In addition, dialogue can be expanded. The PLA is reportedly open to expanding dialogues to lower-level officers. The MMCA, for example, has been praised by the PLA not for its discussion of technical maritime issues but "because it brings U.S. and PLA military officers at the O-5 to O-7 levels where strategic issues can be discussed and 'mutual understanding' pursued."[5]

At a minimum, the U.S. military and the PLA should conduct regular high-level talks. These talks could be meetings involving the Secretary of Defense, Deputy Secretary of Defense, and Under Secretaries or Assistant Secretaries of Defense. Members of the Joint Chiefs of Staff and other general and flag-grade officers from the uniformed services may also be appropriate. Topics of discussion could include

---

[4] Finkelstein and Unangst, pp. 37–38.

[5] Finkelstein and Unangst, p. 40.

the strategic intentions of each country and the policies and concerns of the respective countries toward specific topics, such as Taiwan, proliferation, North Korea, and the GWOT.

Some communication activities can serve as a barometer of the relationship. Examples might range from the symbolic, such as ship visits, to the practical, such as assisting the PLA in environmental cleanup. These types of communications signal to China that the United States does not consider it to be an enemy and provide opportunities for the United States to engage in activities solely to its own benefit, such as searching for the remains of U.S. servicemen. Ship visits, for example, are not prohibited and may be a good mechanism for improving relations. The PLA views ship visits as "both enhancing understanding and symbolizing mutual trust."[6] Using Hong Kong as a transit point for U.S. military ships and aircraft can also communicate U.S. military satisfaction with the military relationship. Continuing port visits and transiting of aircraft by the United States signifies that the United States considers Hong Kong to be a separate administrative region of China that is treated differently from the mainland, in accordance with the agreement signed by Britain and China permitting Hong Kong to retain its economic system and way of life for 50 years after the handover in 1997. Although ship visits and using Hong Kong as a transit point can be viewed as largely symbolic, the PLA does view these types of activities as a signal of U.S. satisfaction or dissatisfaction with the relationship. By carrying out these activities, the U.S. military signals its willingness to take part in other activities to improve the relationship and can help show that the U.S. military does not consider China to be an enemy.

Finally, communication should not be viewed as a channel for building influence or personal bonds of friendship that can be used in a crisis. Expecting such ties to perform these functions is probably misguided; they have failed in the past and will probably fail again. Instead, the ultimate goal of communication is to dissuade the PLA

---

[6] Finkelstein and Unangst, p. 18.

and its civilian leadership from taking courses of action inimical to U.S. interests and disabuse them of misperceptions.

Information Gathering. The second function of a military activities program should be to learn more about China and the PLA. One forum is military education exchanges conducted by military education institutions, such as the military academies, National War College, and National Defense University, with their counterparts in the PLA. As mentioned earlier, part of the value of these types of exchanges is that they provide opportunities for U.S. military officers who have little or no knowledge of China to travel and see the country for themselves rather than rely on second-hand accounts. In addition, this is one area where the U.S. military may benefit more than the PLA. In the U.S. system, strategy and doctrine are developed by the warfighters and are then studied by those in academia. In the Chinese system, strategy and doctrine are first theorized and developed by the military education system. Thus, by conducting military education exchanges with the PLA, it may be possible to gain a window on the development of PLA doctrine and strategy that may provide useful insights into PLA warfighting.

Information gathering can also apply to the attaché corps in China. Attachés legally collect information on the PLA and should continue to do so.

Track 2 and Track 1.5 discussions are another venue for gathering information. They can be useful to "unofficially" discuss issues and can provide opportunities for participants to find solutions to problems in a forum not restricted by policy. They can also be useful in debunking conspiracy theories by permitting those not employed by the U.S. government to clarify U.S. policy.

Limited Cooperation. To safeguard U.S. national security, cooperation with China in response to threats from third parties cannot be ruled out. The best way to respond to any such threats is through intelligence sharing. The prohibition of release of classified or restricted data by the 2000 NDAA is in context of a national security risk. There may be times, however, when it is in U.S. national interests to share intelligence with the PLA, such as intelligence on terrorist groups. Release of this type of information would not harm U.S. national security. Not sharing this type of intelligence may, in fact, threaten U.S. interests.

Improving the Process

For any military-to-military relationship to be successful it will have to be effectively managed. One area to improve upon is planning. Proper planning increases the probability of obtaining reciprocity from the Chinese system. By providing enough time to organize a trip, the U.S. military can choose high-value bases and units and negotiate with the PLA for permission to visit and the level of access. Organizing a trip six to nine months in advance can also potentially alleviate PLA concerns over secrecy. One reason for Chinese reticence in being more open about their activities is that the PLA is governed by a set of restrictive secrecy laws in which the Chinese feel more comfortable not talking than risk violating the law. If the U.S. military requests a visit to a particular location or a briefing on a particular topic and submits questions beforehand, the PLA can prepare presentations and vet them for security. By allowing time for a proper security review, senior officers can approve the parameters of a discussion, permiting their subordinates to discuss the topic more freely. One experienced interlocutor states this has been done on certain occasions and has worked well.

A second way in which proper planning increases transparency and reciprocity is to make sure itineraries provide adequate time to accomplish goals or make sure goals can be met by the trip. Proper planning increases the chances that U.S. delegations are properly staffed, receive adequate briefings, conduct themselves in ways that maximize the ability of the United States to gather information, and are properly debriefed. For example, before a delegation travels to China, members should receive briefings on the state of the overall bilateral relationship, biographical information on expected Chinese counterparts, information and information gaps on specific facilities and units, and the purpose and goals of the trip, including specific questions that should be asked. During the trip, delegation members should be encouraged to ask sensitive questions and should conduct themselves in ways that give them more opportunities to ask questions and receive answers. Delegations should not be staffed by people who are close to retirement unless they also bring replacements. This demonstrates seriousness to the PLA and exposes the incoming leader to the PLA. When the trip is finished, at least one member of the delegation should be required to write a trip report that summarizes the group's experience. This report should be made available in channels that can be accessed by anyone with a need to know. Finally, the U.S. government needs to continue to develop a qualified pool of China analysts to assess the information collected through military-to-military activities.

Getting the PLA to Cooperate

If the U.S. Defense Department can improve the system for handling military-to-military exchanges, will the PLA agree to and implement functional activities to the satisfaction of the U.S. military? Unfortunately, the track record is certainly mixed. Even during the 1980s when the U.S.-China military relationship was at its most robust and when the goals of the United States and China with regard to the world situation and their responses to it were in general agreement, the PLA was still reluctant to provide equal access to its facilities. Current Chinese suggestions to "improve mutual trust" include discussing military contingency plans for the Korean peninsula, which is counter to U.S. national interests. Similarly, full acceptance of the tenets of China's New Security Concept would reduce U.S. global influence. But China is most worried about Taiwan. The Taiwan issue has plagued the military relationship from the outset and continues to be a major impediment to a fundamentally stable overall bilateral relationship. It is also the issue that has the most likelihood of bringing the two countries into armed conflict. Thus, without a resolution of the Taiwan issue, the two sides will remain potential enemies, making it doubtful that high levels of reciprocity and transparency can be achieved.

Failing the establishment of mutual trust, however, are there other ways to manage functional exchanges to incentivize the PLA to be more transparent and reciprocal? If, as analysis indicates, the PLA does value functional exchanges for their benefit in assisting reform, then the U.S. military may be able to strike a deal with the PLA. In exchange for access to the U.S. military, the PLA would have to offer genuine access to its facilities. If either side failed to offer genuine access, then either side could cancel or postpone the exchanges. However, U.S. legal restrictions may preclude achieving this type of deal. The content of any functional exchange that would be valued by the PLA would most likely improve its ability to conduct combat operations and could be interpreted as creating a national security risk to the United States. Thus, a strict interpretation of the 2000 NDAA military-to-military restrictions would render functional visits of little value to the PLA. The U.S. military would not be permitted to provide information of value to the PLA, and in the spirit of reciprocity and transparency, the PLA would in turn provide information of little value to the U.S. military. Thus, in an ironic twist, secrecy on the part of United States, and not China, could be responsible for derailing the implementation of successful functional visits to PLA facilities.

If such an agreement could be established, however, the U.S. military would have to determine what kind of reciprocity would be carried out. One example might be that if one side visits a certain type of facility, then the other side would have similar access to the same type of facility. Another example is "value-based reciprocity"— each side visits facilities that are not necessarily of the same type but are of the same importance. Under this type of exchange, a U.S. military delegation could visit an Su-27 base whereas a PLA delegation could receive briefings on logistics. Value-based reciprocity would reduce the chances of seeing a facility that is of little importance and would allow better metrics to be used in assessing the status and progress of functional exchanges.

The U.S. military faces many hurdles—legal, bureaucratic, and the PLA—in maximizing the benefit of functional exchanges. Any of them could hinder effective implementation of the exchanges. Unresolved challenges in any one of the three areas could reduce the utility of pursuing reciprocity and transparency and probably makes a fully reciprocal functional exchange program unobtainable. This is not to say functional exchanges are intrinsically of low value. Such exchanges are, in fact, of potentially high value, but until the PLA demonstrates that it is prepared to respond in kind to U.S. openness and U.S. legal restrictions are eased, then attempts to achieve openness will most likely fail. Furthermore, restricting military-to-military relations for a reciprocity goal with a low chance of achievement may not be useful when considering the benefits of other types of military-to-military activities. In this case, the best way of dealing with the reciprocity and transparency issue is to remove it as an issue.

Concluding Remarks

The restrictions on military-to-military relations with the PLA served a useful purpose in forcing a review of the U.S.-PLA ties. There is no evidence that curtailing these relations harmed U.S. national security. However, indefinitely curtailing them might have done so. The proposed program recognizes the overall benefits and inherent challenges in the U.S. military relationship with China and delimits a slate of activities designed to assure regional allies, deter Chinese civilian and military leadership, and gather information on the PLA. It is modest and manageable, can be successfully carried out under the present political, military, and legal constraints, and is able to meet its goals. It does not attempt to change China, because China is most likely resistant to U.S. military-imposed change. It is limited in its attempt to influence China, because more robust attempts have failed. It sees the relationship for what it is: strategic competitors who are potential enemies. In this sense, the program is not about security cooperation, because there are few areas in which the U.S. military and the PLA can effectively cooperate. Rather, it is a program of *security management* that provides basic mechanisms for avoiding and resolving conflict. It allows both sides opportunities to communicate policies and concerns, including those areas where the two countries may come into conflict. It permits a modest amount of information gathering and acknowledges that basic relations must be maintained between the two countries to communicate to the Chinese that they are not considered an enemy. It also enables the United States to conduct activities that solely benefit itself and are flexible enough to allow the

U.S. military to cooperate with the PLA when it is essential to broader U.S. national security.

Considering the history of the military relationship with China and the level of suspicion between the two countries, any reinvigoration of military ties should be measured and acknowledge the suspicions and concerns of both sides. Efforts to force a certain set of activities onto the PLA may result in frustration and recrimination. Not forcing the relationship will allow both sides to become comfortable with working with each other, enable the U.S. Defense Department to review and, if necessary, alter future activities in response to PLA implementation, and allow the office responsible for implementing the program a proper workload so that U.S. delegations can maximize the usefulness of each activity. It will also lay a more stable foundation for future military-to-military activities.

Finally, the United States should have realistic expectations of the relationship. U.S. officials should expect negotiations to be tough and prolonged and that the PLA will extract as many concessions from the U.S. military as it can. The United States should therefore set modest goals for the relationship. Considering that China has not renounced the use of force against Taiwan and that the United States has promised "to do whatever it takes" to defend Taiwan, if the U.S. military can ensure that U.S. policies and concerns are understood by the PLA, then the relationship can be considered a success.

Bibliography

Allen, Kenneth, "China's Aviation Capabilities," paper presented at Chinese Military Affairs: a Conference on the State of the Field, sponsored by the National Defense University, October 26–27, 2000.

_____, "U.S.-China Military Relations Not a One-Way Street," *Stimson Center News Advisory*, December 13, 1999.

Allen, Kenneth W., and Eric A. McVadon, *China's Foreign Military Relations*, Henry L. Stimson Center, October 1999.

"An Interview With Teng Hsiao-p'ing," *Time*, February 5, 1979.

Associated Press, "Big-Computer Sale to Soviet Is Barred," June 24, 1977.

Barling, Russel, "China Joins U.S. Drive to Secure Container Trade; Shanghai and Shenzhen Are the First Mainland Ports to Sign the Initiative," *South China Morning Post*, July 30, 2003.

Bradsher, Keith, "U.S. Will Release Weapons to China," *New York Times*, December 23, 1992.

Brzezinski, Zbigniew, *Power and Principle: Memoirs of the National Security Adviser 1977–1981*, New York: Farrar, Straus, Giroux, 1983.

"Bush Vows 'To Do Whatever It Takes' To Defend Taiwan," *CNN.com*, April 25, 2001.

Carter, Ashton, and William J. Perry, *Preventive Defense: A New Security Strategy for America*, Washington, D.C.: Brookings Institution Press, 1999.

Center for Nonproliferation Studies, *China Profiles Database,* "China's Missile Assistance and Exports to Iran," http://www.nti.org/db/china/miranpos.htm.

_____, "China's Nuclear Exports and Assistance to Iran," http://www.nti.org/db/china/miranpos.htm.

_____, *Treaty on the Nonproliferation of Nuclear Weapons*, http://www.nti. org/e_research/official_docs/inventory/pdfs/npt.pdf.

"China's Minister to Pakistan," Pakistan Newswire, September 18, 2001.

"China's Stance and Diplomatic Effort To Solve Iraq Issue," *People's Daily* (online), March 3, 2003.

"China Strongly Protests U.S. Arms Sales to Taiwan," *People's Daily* (online), April 25, 2001.

"China Summons U.S. Ambassador to Make Representations," *People's Daily* (online), March 18, 2002.

"China Urges Japan to Be Prudent In Aiding Fight Against Terrorism," *People's Daily* (online), September 28, 2001.

"Chinese, U.S. Presidents Talk Over Phone," *People's Daily* (online), September 13, 2001.

"Facts and Figures: China's Top Ten Trade Partners in 2001," *People's Daily* (online), February 13, 2002.

Finkelstein, David M., *China's New Security Concept: Reading Between the Lines*, Alexandria, VA: Center for Naval Analyses Corporation, April 1999.

Finkelstein, David M., and John Unangst, *Engaging DoD: Chinese Perspectives on Military Relations with the United States*, Alexandria, VA: Center for Naval Analyses Corporation, October 1999.

"FM Spokesman: Chinese Government Condemns Terrorism," *People's Daily* (online), September 12, 2001.

Frieman, Wendy, "New Members of the Club: Chinese Participation in Arms Control Regimes 1980–1995," *Nonproliferation Review*, Spring/Summer 1996.

Gellman, Barton, "Reappraisal Led to New China Policy; Skeptics Abound, But U.S. 'Strategic Partnership' Yielding Results," *Washington Post*, June 22, 1998.

Gertz, Bill, "China's New Era at Pentagon; 'Red Carpet' Rolled Out to General Tainted by Massacre," *Washington Times*, August 18, 1994.

_____, "Panel Clips Perry's Wings, Bars Links to China's Military," *Washington Times*, May 29, 1995.

_____, "Chinese Generals Visit Draws Fire; Pelosi Rips Honors for Tiananmen Massacre Architect," *Washington Times*, November 26, 1996.

_____, "Military Exchanges with Beijing Raises Security Concerns," *Washington Times*, February 19, 1999.

_____, "General Postpones Trip to China," *Washington Times*, March 22, 1999.

_____, "Helms Calls for Less Exchange with China," *Washington Times*, March 26, 1999.

_____, "General Postpones China Trip," *Washington Times,* March 22, 1999.

_____, "Chinese Visit Sensitive Military Facilities," *Washington Times*, August 24, 2000.

Get, Jer Donald, "What's with the Relationship Between America's Army and China's PLA?" *Strategic Studies Institute*, September 15, 1996.

Gill, Bates, and Evan S. Medeiros, "The Foreign and Domestic Influences on China's Arms Control and Nonproliferation Policies," *China Quarterly*, March 2000.

Gordon, Michael R., "Rumsfeld Limiting Military Contacts with the Chinese," *New York Times*, June 4, 2001.

Gwertzman, Bernard, "Brzezinski Gave Details to China on Arms Talks with Soviet Union," *New York Times*, May 28, 1978.

_____, "U.S. Reported Acting to Strengthen Ties with Peking Regime," *New York Times*, June 26, 1978.

Harding, Harry, *A Fragile Relationship: The United States and China Since 1972,* Washington, D.C.: The Brookings Institution, 1992.

Higgins, Andrew, and Charles Hutzler, "Chinese Goals Take a Backseat as U.S. Rises to the Fore in Asia," *Wall Street Journal*, October 19, 2001.

Information Office of the State Council of the People's Republic of China, *China's National Defense in 2002*, December 9, 2002.

_____, *China's National Defense in 2000*, October 16, 2000.

_____, *China's National Defense*, July 1998.

International Intellectual Property Alliance web page release.

Jiang Lei, *Xiandai yilie shengyou zhanlue* [Modern Strategy of Using the Inferior to Defeat the Superior], Chinese Military Science Ph.D. Dissertation Series, National Defense University, 1997.

Jin, Canrong, "Great Power Relations from a Comparative Perspective," *Xiandai Guoji Guanxi*, March 20, 2002.

Kaplan, Brad, "China and U.S.: Building Military Relations," *Asia-Pacific Defense Forum* (online), Summer 1999.

Keefe, John, "A Tale of 'Two Very Sorries' Redux," *Far Eastern Economic Review* (online), March 21, 2002.

La Croix, Sumner J., and Denise Eby Konan, "Intellectual Property Rights in China: The Changing Political Economy of Chinese-American Interests," *The World Economy*, June 2002.

Lampton, David M., and Richard Daniel Ewing, *U.S.-China Relations in a Post–September 11th World,* Washington, D.C.: The Nixon Center, 2002.

Lardner Jr., George, and Jeffrey Smith, "Intelligence Ties Endure Despite U.S.-China Strain; 'Investment' Is Substantial, Longstanding," *Washington Post*, June 25, 1989.

Liu, Jianfei, "Listen for 'Fizz'—Empires Decline Not with Bang But with Fizz; Unilateralism Is Equally Dangerous to United States," *Shijie Zhishi*, May 1, 2002.

Mann, Jim, "Administration Urged to Renew China Defense Ties; Diplomacy: U.S. Needs Military Contacts to Keep Abreast of Beijing's Arms Sales, Buildups, Officials Say," *Los Angeles Times*, March 7, 1993.

McMillan, Zlex Frew, and Major Garrett, "U.S. Wins Support From China," *CNN.com*, October 19, 2001.

Medeiros, Evan S., "Through a Red Glass Darkly," *Far Eastern Economic Review*, November 9, 2000.

_____, "Integrating a Rising Power into Global Nonproliferation Regimes: U.S.-China Negotiations and Interactions on Nonproliferation, 1980–2001," unpublished Ph.D. dissertation, London: London School of Economics, July 2002.

Mufson, Steven, "U.S. to Help China Retool Arms Plants; Perry Received as 'Old Friend' in Quest of Military Ties; Human Rights Discussed," *Washington Post,* October 18, 1994.

"Musharaff Says Complete Unanimity of Sino-Pak Views on Key Issues, Pakistan Newswire, December 25, 2001.

Myers, Steven Lee, "Chinese Military to Resume Contacts With the Pentagon," *New York Times*, January 6, 2000.

Niu, Jun, "Shocks Bring About Change," *Xiandai Guoji Guanxi*, March 20, 2002.

"No Double Standards in Anti-Terror Fight, Says China of Domestic Unrest," *AFP,*October 11, 2001.

North, Oliver, *Under Fire: An American Story*, New York: HarperCollins 1991.

Pan, Phillip P., "China Issues Rules on Missile Exports," *Washington Post,* August 25, 2002.

Perry, William H., "U.S. Strategy: Engage China, Not Contain It," remarks delivered to the Washington State China Relations Council, October 30, 1995.

Pollack, Jonathan, *The Lessons of Coalition Politics: Sino-American Security Relations*, Santa Monica: RAND Corporation, 1984.

Pomfret, John, "Pentagon Talks May Lead to More U.S.-China Military Cooperation, Joint Exercises," *Washington Post,* December 12, 1997.

_____, "Cohen Hails Achievements in China Visit; Halt in Missile Sales to Iran, Closer Military Ties Cited," *Washington Post*, January 20, 1998.

"Powell Praises China's Role in Reducing Indo-Pakistan Tensions," *Press Trust of India*, April 25, 2002.

Pu, Qibi, "The U.S. Has Profited From 9.11," *Shijie Zhishi*, May 1, 2002.

Shalal-Esa, Andrea, "U.S. Vows to Do What It Takes to Aid Taiwan Defense," *Reuters*, April 9, 2002.

Shalikashvili, John M., "Remarks to PLA National Defense University on U.S.-China Engagement: The Role of Military-to-Military Contacts," May 14, 1997.

Shambaugh, David, "Sino-American Strategic Relations: From Partners to Competitors," *Survival*, Spring 2000.

Swaine, Michael D., and Ashley J. Tellis, *Interpreting China's Grand Strategy: Past, Present and Future*, MR-1121-AF, Santa Monica: RAND Corporation, 2000.

"Taiwan Says Armitage's Clarification on U.S. Policy Conducive to Regional Peace," *British Broadcasting Corporation*, August 27, 2002.

Tyler, Patrick, *A Great Wall: Six Presidents and China*, New York: The Century Foundation, 1999.

United Nations, *United Nations Security Council Resolution 1441*, November 8, 2002.

U.S. Department of Defense, "Secretary of Defense William Perry, Memorandum for the Secretaries of the Army, Navy and Air Force Concerning the U.S.-China Military Relationship," July 1994.

_____, DoD News Briefing, January 18, 1996.

_____, DoD News Briefing, January 20, 1998.

_____, Secretary of Defense William S. Cohen News Briefing, July 13, 2000.

_____, *Proliferation: Threat and Response*, January 2001.

_____, Letter to Representative Bob Stump from Paul Wolfowitz on military-to-military exchanges with the People's Liberation Army, June 8, 2001.

_____, *Quadrennial Defense Review*, September 30, 2001.

_____, *Report of Past Military to Military Exchanges and Contacts Between the U.S. and PRC*, undated.

_____, "Deputy Secretary Wolfowitz Interview With Phoenix Television," *Defense Department News Transcript*, May 31, 2002.

_____, *Annual Report on the Military Power of the People's Republic of China*, July 12, 2002.

_____, General Tommy Franks press briefing, April 11, 2002.

_____, "Under Secretary Feith Media Roundtable on U.S. China Defense Consultative Talks," *Defense Department News Transcript*, December 9, 2002.

U.S. Department of State, *Global Patterns of Terrorism 2001*, May 21, 2002.

"U.S. Envoy Hails 'Resolute' China But Denies Xinjiang Terror Claims," Deutsche Presse-Agentur, December 6, 2001.

Weinraub, Bernard, "U.S. Study Sees Peril in Selling Arms to China," *New York Times*, June 24, 1977.

White House, *The National Security Strategy of the United States of America*, September 2002.

_____, "President Bush Meets with Chinese President Jiang Zemin," White House press release, February 21, 2002.

_____, "Fact Sheet: Accomplishments of U.S.-China Summit," October 29, 1997.

_____, "U.S., China Stand Against Terrorism, Remarks by President Bush and President Jiang Zemin," White House press release, October 19, 2001.

_____, "Presidential Review Memorandum/NSC 24."

Wilborn, Thomas L., "Security Cooperation with China: Analysis and a Proposal," *U.S. Army War College*, November 25, 1994.

Williams, Daniel, "China Finds 'Comprehensive Engagement' Hard to Grasp," *Washington Post*, February 13, 1995.

Williams Daniel, and R. Jeffrey Smith, "U.S. to Renew Contact with Chinese Military; Meeting Reflects Strategy of Easing Tension," *Washington Post*, November 1, 1993.